"It has been fun working with David. I have learned so many new things about swing fundamentals and how the body and muscles work. I'm excited about what lies ahead, and you will be, too, if you try David's A Swing—it could really help your game."

—Lydia Ko, world's #1 female golfer
and multiple LPGA Tour winner

"The A Swing represents a genuine breakthrough in the realm of golf instruction. Uncomplicated in its philosophy and with scientific proof of its effectiveness, the A Swing has the potential to make a significant difference to the way in which the game is taught and played—and, indeed, the speed at which regular golfers can begin to enjoy hitting consistently solid shots. With characteristically astute observation, the world's most innovative teaching professional has delivered a major contribution to the game of golf."

—Richard Simmons, editor of *Golf International Magazine* (UK)

"I am a junior golfer who was not making much headway in the game. The A Swing gave me a plan, and within a few months I went from being an 80 shooter to shooting in the 60s. I just stick to the plan and don't deviate. I know I am going to have a successful college career and hopefully someday compete on the PGA Tour."

—Kymer Li, junior golfer

"I have been a passionate, competitive senior golfer for many years. When David introduced me to the A Swing, it made all the difference. It is so understandable and answered all my questions. My consistency has improved immensely, and it makes practicing more productive. The A Swing has given me a new lease on life, and I know I can still improve and hopefully win many more tournaments."

—Arlene McKitrick, senior golfer and
winner of more than 200 tournaments

"I am a new golfer and learned to play using the A Swing. My friends are amazed by how well I hit the ball already. The A Swing is easy to understand and makes absolute sense. All amateurs should try it."

—Pete Simonson, novice golfer

"This A Swing is simple and efficient, easy to repeat, and has allowed me to play well despite my back issues. I don't have to practice as much, and my misses have been so much better. You need to try it!"

—Ryan Blaum, leading money-winner
at the 2013 PGA Latin American Tour

"After many years of practicing and searching for the key to the swing, I believe this is it. The A Swing is awesome, simple, and easy to apply. Wish I knew about this twenty-five years ago!"

—Denis Watson, three-time PGA Tournament winner
and winner of the 2007 PGA Senior Championship

"Trying the A Swing was an amazing transformation. My game was so inconsistent, but in just a few shots of working with this different backswing, I started hitting the ball out of the middle of the clubface and really striping it. My golf buddies were blown away by how much accuracy and distance I gained!"   —Jackie Flynn (8 handicap), actor and comedian

"The A Swing I have worked on with David is so easy to do and repeat, and when it goes off I have a clear picture of what to do to get back on track."

—Alex Levy (France), two-time European Tour winner

"My technique since working with David has improved amazingly. The A Swing is very natural, I don't have to overthink it, and the world's greatest golfer incorporated parts of it. I feel I can now reach my true potential as a player."   —Rafael Cabrera-Bello (Spain),
two-time European Tour winner

"I struggled toward the end of my junior golf career, but since working on the A Swing with David, things have really turned around. I feel my swing is so manageable now that I only have to see David for a few minutes periodically to keep it on track. I am looking forward to a successful LPGA career."   —Simin Feng (China), newly turned professional golfer
and winner of the 2014 SEC College Championship

"There is a wonderful simplicity and logic to the A Swing, which produced instant results in my game, making range time meaningful and giving my confidence a huge boost on the course in competition. One of the keys to playing better golf is 'trusting your swing,' entertaining no self-doubt and having a firm conviction that it will work as required, especially under pressure. The A Swing does what it says on the tin! The scientifically proven biomechanical advantage of this swing speaks for itself, and I can say without doubt it has made the single greatest positive impact on my game in forty years."   —Robin Sieger, peak performance coach and
author of the bestselling *Silent Mind Golf*

"As a sixty-plus-year-old golfer with a low handicap, my performance had plateaued. I had taken many lessons over the years, but nothing has been as logical and clear as the A Swing. The A Swing has renewed my interest in the game, as it has enabled me to perform well in competition. I am hitting it longer, and my shot dispersion has improved significantly. There is less stress on my body, and golf is more fun. An antiaging system if ever there was one!"

—Dr. Joe Branconi, senior golfer

"David is a credit to golf. He loves the game as much as anybody I have ever seen, and the A Swing may be one of the greatest contributions. If there is a better teacher in golf than David, I would like to meet him."

—Gary Player, 165 tournament wins, 9 majors, 9 senior majors, and the career Grand Slam

THE A SWING

THE ALTERNATIVE APPROACH TO GREAT GOLF

DAVID LEADBETTER

WITH **Ron Kaspriske**

FOREWORD BY MICHELLE WIE

ST. MARTIN'S GRIFFIN ❧ NEW YORK

This book is dedicated to my family—

my wife, Kelly, and children, Andy, Hally, and James—

who always inspire me to be the best.

Published in the United States by St. Martin's Griffin, an imprint of St. Martin's Publishing Group

THE A SWING. Copyright © 2015 by David Leadbetter. Foreword copyright © 2015 by Michelle Wie. All rights reserved. Printed in Singapore. For information, address St. Martin's Publishing Group, 120 Broadway, New York, NY 10271.

www.stmartins.com

Designed by Richard Oriolo

The Library of Congress has cataloged the hardcover edition as follows:

Leadbetter, David.
  The a swing : the alternative approach to great golf / David Leadbetter with Ron Kaspriske.
     pages cm
   ISBN 978-1-250-06491-2 (hardback)—ISBN 978-1-4668-7145-8 (ebook) 1. Swing (Golf) I. Kaspriske, Ron. II. Title.
  GV979.S9L423 2015
  796.352'3—dc23

2015007272

ISBN 978-1-250-80506-5 (trade paperback)

Our books may be purchased for promotional, educational, or business use. Please contact your local bookseller or the Macmillan Corporate and Premium Sales Department at 1-800-221-7945, extension 5442, or by email at MacmillanSpecialMarkets@macmillan.com.

First St. Martin's Griffin Edition: 2021

10 9 8 7 6 5 4 3 2 1

CONTENTS

FOREWORD

DAVID LEADBETTER HAS BEEN MY golf instructor since I was thirteen years old, and when I think back on our countless practice sessions and tournaments working together, our greatest successes came from our shared passion to reach my goals. At times in my career, setbacks and injuries have dampened my desire to practice and play. I bet you've had bouts of frustration with golf, too. Believe me, I know how infuriating this game can be. But instead of letting those frustrations get the best of me, we focused on that passion for the game, and that helped me win the U.S. Open at Pinehurst in 2014. Obviously, I felt nervous in trying to win that tournament—especially in the final round. But you know what else I felt? I was excited. I woke up on the morning of the final round and was so excited to get out there and play, with total belief in my abilities. I had a lot of fun. When the tournament was over, I couldn't wait to play the following week. Practice, too. I love going out there hitting balls and working on my game now. So my advice is that if your game has got you down, it's time to make some changes to get your passion for golf back.

One thing that has made golf so much more enjoyable for me is knowing more about my golf swing—it's helped improve my consistency. I'm hitting my driver with confidence. I'm hitting more greens in regulation, and I'm giving myself more chances for birdies. I know I'm more consistent now because my swing has become more efficient and reliable. There's not a lot of wasted motion. I focus on getting into a solid setup, fully coiling my body during the backswing while keeping my arm swing nice and compact. I am then able to swing back down into the ball with everything moving in sync. We've worked hard on these principles, and they are the same fundamentals that make David's A Swing so effective and such a great option for so many golfers.

I've learned from David that no two golf swings are exactly alike, so what matters is finding a way to swing the club that makes it easy to repeatedly hit good golf shots. When I was growing up, I worked hard on my overall game, and my having plenty of power made golf relatively easy for me. But as I got older and my body started to naturally change, so did my swing. Part of the change came from dealing with injuries, but I also started to overthink things. The game became a lot harder as I tried to achieve perfection. But now I know that you can't be perfect. Instead, you should develop a technique, believe in it, work on it, and go out and play the game *your* way. What I have worked on with David is based on efficiency and an understanding of how my own swing works, and I know what to look for if something goes wrong so I can quickly fix it. Trust me when I say that you can't play good golf if you are focusing on swing mechanics the whole time—you have to simplify things. The goal is to be able to stand over the ball and know you're about to hit a solid shot, straight to your target. That's the case now with my swing. Sure I hit some bad shots, as every player does, but I don't worry about losing my swing. I focus on my basics and just go out and play. That's what David's teaching is all about. He's always looking for a simple approach to improve a player's confidence and make the game more enjoyable.

I'm sure many of you know my journey in professional golf has had its ups and downs. But David and I never gave up on fine-tuning my game, so that it held up to the scrutiny of a final round in a major. You might never reach that plateau, but I believe you'll find your own level of success if you follow David's advice in this book and give the A Swing a try. If you do, I know you will have less frustration and you'll find it a lot easier to play consistent golf. Now go make some birdies!

—Michelle Wie

I've been teaching this game for over forty years and have worked with golfers of all abilities. It doesn't matter whether I'm coaching someone trying to win a major championship (I've coached nineteen major championship winners), or someone that simply wants to break 100; for me the thrill has always been to see that golfer succeed. That's why I've developed a different approach to swinging the club. I call it the A Swing, as in the *alternative* swing. The A Swing follows sound scientific principles; while visually it does not appear that different from a traditional swing, it is a far easier way to hit the ball consistently. I created it out of empathy for golfers who have struggled to reach their goals with traditional swing techniques. In the ensuing chapters, I will detail what makes it work, how simple

INTRODUCTION

it is to learn, and why it might just be your key to playing consistently better golf. Before I get to that, let me further explain why I developed the A Swing.

I believe golf is the most difficult sport to master. You might for a while have the recipe to playing well, but it never seems to last. One day the swing feels smooth and effortless—the ball is sweetly struck and the shots are consistent. The next day, the motion can feel awkward and labored—the ball seems to go anywhere but where you intend. This fuels both the mystery and allure of golf; we are not sure what to expect. It happens to all golfers—the complexity of the game makes it tough to be consistent, especially at the recreational level. Why is this, and why do we put ourselves through this kind of stress playing the game? What keeps us coming back? I think it's because it is so exhilarating to hit a well-struck golf shot, where the swing feels fluid and everything goes right. Despite the game's numerous complexities—from the physical requirements of the golf swing; to being in the right frame of mind; to the dizzying equipment options; to the ever-changing weather conditions; to the varying course layouts, grasses, and lies; to the sheer number of different shots that need to be learned—we somehow, sometimes, find a way to execute good shots. Every time we tee it up, we live in hope that this happens. Why is the game so elusive, we often ask ourselves.

Most golfers have learned through experience that their times of hitting the ball consistently well are fleeting. These are soon replaced by the times of frustration at playing poorly. I think that's the real issue for most golfers. They know they can hit good shots and play well at times, but are so inconsistent they get frustrated, not knowing what they're doing wrong, trying several fixes, and often going from bad to worse. Even if they do know what the problem is, they typically don't have enough time to fix it. The pros have the advantage that aside from their talent, they practice for dozens of hours every week, more than a thousand hours each year, working on repetition. Most everyone else who plays the game simply cannot afford that time commitment. And don't forget, even if amateurs do find the time for practice, a lot of it should be spent on the all-important short game.

The odd lesson, swing tip, or equipment change can help make up for that lack of time, but statistics show that most recreational players don't improve because they can't put the hours in to perfect the traditional approach to swinging a club. Even more troubling is that the more golfers become aggravated with their game, the less desire they have to play and practice. Think of how frustrating it is to invest time, effort, and money on something you care about, but get nothing in return except poor results. So I believe what this game needs is a simpler way of swinging the club that will help the majority of golfers get results without the countless hours of practice.

Over the decades, I've seen a lot of developments in how the game is taught and what is used to teach it—high-speed video cameras, three-dimensional analysis software, launch monitors, psychological training, golf-related workouts, personalized club-fitting, adjustable equipment, etc. All these advances have come in the hopes of making golf easier and improving the standard. But in reality, the standard has not improved. Certainly the level of play is better than ever at the top of the game—the professional tours and the best amateur and junior competitions. There are far more elite players now than ever before in the history of golf. But playing consistently good golf is still extremely difficult for 95 percent of the game's participants. That's because it's hard to repetitively put the clubface squarely on the ball and hit it to the target without a real commitment to lessons and practice. Even then for those who do devote the time, there are still no guarantees.

While this notion might be sobering, it's undeniable. Why is the golf swing so difficult to master? There are a lot of reasons, but one of the biggest is, you start from a fairly static position and have to make a pretty big movement to swing the club back to hit a stationary ball. How could it be more difficult than trying to hit a moving object the way you're required to do in such sports as tennis, baseball, or hockey? Believe it or not, it is harder. At least that's been my experience in working with natural athletes who start playing golf after excelling in other sports. For one thing, in other sports the margin of error is far greater. In tennis, you always get two chances to serve the ball over the net. In baseball, think of how many times it's acceptable for a batter to miss a pitch or foul one off before successfully getting a hit. The foul balls in golf come with far greater consequences. Adding to the difficulty of golf is the tension and overthinking that occurs before the swing even starts. When you swing a bat, racquet, or hockey stick, you typically start in rhythm and have a relatively short, uncomplicated backswing as compared to golf, as you instinctively react to hit a moving object. There's little time, if any, for fear, negative thoughts, or too many technical thoughts to creep into your mind. Your natural athletic ability takes over. But in golf, there seems to be all the time in the world to overthink the situation and the technique! The ball is just sitting there. There's nothing to react to. In these moments, golfers' conscious minds take over their natural instincts, and their chances of hitting a good shot are reduced.

Knowing this, and the myriad of other reasons why golf is so difficult, I decided it was important to develop a technical way to swing the club that is more efficient, simple, and repeatable, that once mastered, doesn't require you to think too much. A way that makes your swing fluid, helps you to generate what I call easy power, and just as important, if not more so, to hit the ball more accurately. After all our testing of players of all abilities, and seeing their levels of consistency drastically improve, I think the A Swing could in reality stand for "the Accuracy Swing"! The A Swing allows you to tap into your natural athletic ability that makes other ball-and-stick sports so much easier to play.

I've seen many swings that work and many that don't. A golf swing that works doesn't have to be pleasing to the eye. Ernie Els, whom I coached for many years, has exquisite rhythm and swings the club beautifully—it's poetry in motion. But just as effective as Ernie's swing is the unorthodox method of Jim Furyk (which ironically has somewhat of a small resemblance to the A Swing). The reason is, just like Ernie, Jim can consistently hit the ball on the club's sweet spot. Their successes should tell you that the eye often doesn't see what is repeatable in good swings. Striking the ball solidly and consistently is all about the efficient and sequential transfer of energy from one part of the body to the next. It's how the energy flows from the lower body up to the shoulders, down the arms, through the hands, and finally into a powerful release of the clubhead. The science of biomechanics sheds light on what is happening in the golf swing. In the following chapter, my longtime associate J. J. Rivet of Biomecaswing, one of the world's leading experts on athletic motions, will explain the science behind the A Swing. His analysis shows that it allows many golfers, particularly the recreational player, to make a simpler, more effective, and repeatable swing than if they swung in a more traditional way.

Also lending his expertise to why the A Swing works is my good friend Steven Yellin, author of *The Fluid Motion Factor*. He teaches students how to access the part of the brain that lets them perform any sport at an optimum level. On reviewing the A Swing, Steven said it works because it adheres to one of nature's most accepted practices—the principle of least effort. Nature is always operating with a goal of doing as little as possible to complete a task, and the A Swing demonstrates this ethos.

All great players when performing at their best are supremely efficient with their motion. For example, we all marvel at Freddy Couples's, Ernie Els's, or Rory McIlroy's swings because they look effortless and produce so much power. The same was true of legendary ice hockey player Wayne Gretzky, whose skating always appeared effortless. Because of his small stature, he had to be efficient with his movement, so he learned how to skate not to where the puck was, but where the puck was going to be. Yellin also reminded me of a great article written in 2006 in *The New York Times Magazine* entitled "Roger Federer as a Religious Experience." In the article, the author said that watching Federer play tennis was like watching perfection in motion. He was never out of position, never looked rushed. He generated tremendous racquet speed with what appeared to be little effort.

"Top athletes embody the principle of least effort," Yellin says. "The principle behind the A Swing parallels the environment and minimalist framework in which great athletes compete and the universe operates." This book shows you how the A Swing will make your motions simpler and more efficient, resulting in effortless power and better accuracy.

I like to think of the A Swing as an approach or style to playing good golf. It's not a strict method and has some latitude in learning it and executing it. Besides, I've never liked the word *method* when it comes to teaching golf. A method implies there is only one way to swing the club effectively, but as Ernie Els's and Jim Furyk's swings consistently demonstrate, that can't possibly be true. However, all swings that hit the ball consistently well have one commonality—*they're synchronized.* By that I mean there is a harmonious movement of the body, arms, hands, and club—they move in proper sequence at the proper time. If you can sync your body's rotational movement with the swinging action of the arms and club, you're on your way to hitting good shots more often and, just as important for good scoring, to improving the quality of your not-so-good shots. When the ball-striking is off, even for top players, synchronization is normally to blame. It's the essence of the A Swing—to get you synced up! I've found that much of the A Swing's success stems from its ability to help golfers get synced up as never before.

I want to state a few things from the outset. Even though the *A* in *A Swing* stands for "alternative," I think most of you will find by observing a player utilizing the A Swing, or by looking at yourself on video working on it, that the swing does not appear radically different from so-called traditional swing technique. I've taught what could be termed a more conventional approach to the golf swing for decades, but with a definite hint of the A Swing in there, and I assure you, I'm not drifting too far from my roots. This A Swing, through research and testing, is just an evolution of what I've believed in and have been teaching for many years. I'd also like to point out that I don't teach the total A Swing to everyone—certain aspects of it, however, would benefit a great number of players. If you've enjoyed considerable success swinging the club in a more conventional manner and are synced up regularly—if you hit the ball fairly consistently, are lucky enough to have an Adam Scott's raw ability or say a Tiger Woods's power—then you probably don't need the A Swing, but this book will still be a good read! But for a lot of you golfers, I believe the A Swing can make a huge difference. At the end of this chapter I'll detail who I think will benefit the most from using it.

So what makes the A Swing unique? The major difference occurs during the backswing. Golfers and instructors spend a great deal of time trying to develop or correct this part of the swing in the quest to make a good downswing. If you were able to eavesdrop on every golf lesson given around the world, you would probably find that 10 percent of the instruction would be on setup, i.e., grip, posture, alignment, ball position; 10 percent would revolve around the downswing, impact, and finish; and a whopping 80 percent would be focused on the backswing. Doesn't that tell you that the backswing, which we know is so important to set you up for a good downswing, is the problem area in the golf swing? It's the area that golfers have through the eras failed to come to grips with and where most instruction and correction is based. So it seems logical to assume that in many respects the traditional way of going about making a backswing is far too complicated for most golfers to achieve and is the cause of poor golf. The A Swing simplifies things a great deal, making the all-important downswing that much easier to achieve.

Now that you know why I developed the A Swing and what it could do for your game, let me briefly explain how I created it. Its construction was greatly influenced by my work through the years with Sir Nick Faldo and Nick Price, who both have won multi major championships and been world number ones, plus other top men and women players. I gleaned knowledge by studying the athletic motions in sports such as baseball and tennis. Other aspects came from experts in physiology and biomechanics. The underlying principle was to develop a simpler way to take the club back, so that players could make a better downswing by utilizing their torsos more efficiently. Complex backswings lead to an overuse of and reliance on the hands and arms on the downswing at the expense of good body motion—the kind of motions I see average golfers struggling with continuously, affecting power, accuracy, and consistency. Those players never seem to be able to permanently vanquish their bad habits. You might think, why should I give out the recipe for good golf using the A Swing, since the struggles of golfers are what keep my academies worldwide in business! Kidding aside, it's always been my goal to develop an approach to the game that's easy to understand, takes minimal practice, and can be utilized by players of all skill levels for maximum benefit. Now there's a motto: Minimal practice, maximum benefit!

In the following chapters, I'll get down to the nitty-gritty of how and why the A Swing works. For now, I want you to understand that this approach is simple to learn and gives you a better chance to hit good golf shots even in the early stages of learning it. I've found that grasping even only a small portion of the A Swing technique, while working toward mastering it, will help you routinely hit better shots. The closer you come to swinging along the easy-to-follow guidelines, the more effective and consistent your swing will become. All I'll ask is that you keep an open mind—especially if you've taken many lessons over the years and are well versed in traditional golf instruction. In some instances, the A Swing will seem counterintuitive to what you've been taught or know about the golf swing, although I don't think you'll care if it allows you to routinely hit powerful drives and crisp irons. And if you're among the high percentage of golfers who slice the ball, you're going to be amazed how easy it is to straighten that shot out and even curve the ball in the other direction. You'll also have a far greater understanding of how your swing works and, perhaps for the first time, be able to quickly diagnose your problems and fix them.

You might think that the A Swing will only benefit higher-handicap players, but that's not so. I've tested it with players of all skill levels from beginners to tour pros, and the results have been overwhelmingly positive. I'd like to share a couple of testimonials from players whom I've asked to try it. One is from Hollywood comedian Jackie Flynn. Jackie has appeared in many movies, including *There's Something About Mary*. He's a good player and loves the game, but he was struggling in recent years. Only a couple months after I taught the A Swing to him, he called to tell me he had lowered his Handicap Index several strokes (it dropped to as low as 2.7). I could hear the excitement in his voice. "It's the most amazing thing I've ever seen," he told me. "I was immediately hitting the ball twenty yards farther, drawing it with my driver, and I'm two clubs longer with my irons." Even better, he says he's now routinely beating his golf buddies.

Another test case was my old pal Denis Watson. Over the years Denis has won three PGA Tour events, including the World Series of Golf, and a major on the senior tour—the 2007 Senior PGA Championship. Denis has always been a superb ball-striker, and if not blighted by injuries throughout his career, he would probably have gone on to win majors on the regular tour—he did finish second at the 1985 U.S. Open. I talk to him quite a bit and value his feedback about the golf swing. Known as a guy who speaks his mind, Denis recently said to me that the A Swing is so good and makes so much sense, he wondered, "Why didn't you tell me about it earlier in my career?" Sorry, Denis.

I think that everyone from weekend golfers to really good players can benefit from the A Swing. When you also consider that you can learn it in far less time than it takes to try to master traditional swing techniques, it could potentially bring to or keep so many more time-challenged players in the game. I hope that it might get people, particularly instructors, thinking about how the game is being taught. With all due respect to the traditions of golf, it's time to make the game easier to learn and play—to change the paradigm somewhat. Think of all the retired baby boomers and young professionals who would like to get into golf, but have been reluctant to try because it's too difficult to have any success. Think of all the recreational players who constantly struggle and play less and less as a result of losing enjoyment for the game. How about all the aging golfers who are frustrated and depressed about their games because not only have they lost distance, but also consistency? The A Swing can be the answer and salvation for a lot of these people. When golfers start seeing progress and success, they have the incentive to go out and play and practice, and that's what it's all about, isn't it?

In a nutshell, if you're frustrated with your golf, feel that you could be so much better, feel that you have exhausted every avenue to improve, the A Swing is something you should try. Trust me, it works. I like to say to my students, "You may well find your A game with the A Swing."

To help you learn it, I've included a lot of guideposts and over two hundred illustrations in this book. Our model in the book depicting the A Swing wears a red shirt. For easy reference, in illustrations showing faults or a non–A Swing approach he wears a black shirt. I identify common faults and show you how the A Swing corrects them. I also offer you tips, practice drills, and things you should feel and visualize to speed up learning. For easy reference, at the end of each section in the technique chapters, I conclude with a "Nuggets" segment, with the symbol 🝙, a summary of the main points we have covered. In the arms-and-club-movement chapter, which explains where the A Swing really differs from the traditional approach, (particularly the backswing), are "Frequently Asked Questions" sections, based on questions posed to me from students we have tested. All of this adds up to having a complete toolbox to help you learn the A Swing. Note that all of the instructions in this book assume the player who is learning the A Swing is right-handed. If you're a lefty, I apologize for this inconvenience, but I did this to simplify the instructions. I hope you're used to having to make the necessary right-to-left conversions when looking at golf instruction.

With that said, I have one more piece of good news. Actually, I've saved the best part of the A Swing for last. **You can learn it with an easy-to-follow, seven-minute practice plan.** If you do the program outlined in chapter 7, all it takes is seven minutes a day, a few times a week, and you'll have no problem developing and maintaining the mechanics and feeling for the A Swing. That's significantly more appealing than the many hours of practice you would need to improve using the traditional approach. The short and efficient practice sessions are done indoors without a ball. They'll give you insight into what it feels like to repetitively make a good swing while developing your muscle memory. Certainly even the most time-strapped person can find seven minutes a few times a week to practice. As a bonus, I've included a simple, functional, non-time-consuming A Swing fitness program. These golf-specific movements are easy to do and extremely beneficial for general strength and mobility. They come from our master trainer, Trevor Anderson, who is director of the Leadbetter Performance Program at my academies. If you commit to doing the fitness program semiregularly, it will enhance your ability to play better than ever. And who doesn't want a stronger, more flexible body that is free of aches and pains?

I'm excited about the A Swing because I know the approach works, it's easy to teach and even easier to learn—and it is backed by science. I've seen incredible changes and, in most cases, immediate improvement in the golfers who have tested it. I've dedicated my life to teaching this wonderful game, and my highs come from watching the faces of my students light up after they have hit a well-struck golf shot, and then do it again and again. I know the A Swing will do the same for you. I look forward to our taking this journey together.

—DAVID LEADBETTER

GOLFERS WHO WILL BENEFIT FROM THE A SWING

I'm not naïve enough to think that the A Swing will be universally accepted or will suit every golfer. As I have mentioned, if you already have a well-synchronized swing and can consistently hit solid and accurate shots, why would you want to change? As the cliché goes, "If it ain't broke, don't fix it!" But for a lot of golfers, the A Swing finally offers another option. So here's a list of who I think will most benefit from it:

- **Beginners**

- **Slicers**

- **Golfers whose shots continually finish left of the target no matter how far right they aim**

- **Senior golfers who have lost their flexibility and their power**

- **Golfers who are constantly told that their swings are too fast or too jerky**

- **Women golfers who have long, loose swings as a result of lack of strength and excess flexibility**

- **Juniors with quick body actions, whose arms and torso are out of sync**

- **Players who keep reverting to their old bad habits**

- **Good players whose long game lacks consistency**

- **Players who are erratic off the tee**

- **Players who struggle hitting iron shots solidly and accurately**

- **Golfers who like to tinker with technique and want something new to try**

- **People who are frustrated with their game but don't have a lot of time to work on it**

EDITOR'S NOTE: Biomechanics in sports can be described as the quantifiable muscular, joint, and skeletal actions of the body during the execution of a given task, skill, and/or technique. J.-J. Rivet is one of the world's leading authorities on how the body moves during athletic activities, particularly during the golf swing. He specializes in detecting inefficient movement and offering solutions on how to improve the required action. He has been lecturing on this topic at various universities since 1985, including at Aix-Marseille University and the University of Montpellier in France. J. J. is also a former consultant to the PGA's European Tour. He now conducts his studies at Biomecaswing in France. Here is his analysis of the A Swing.

CHAPTER 1

WHY THE A SWING WORKS —A SCIENTIFIC ANALYSIS

BY J. J. RIVET, BIOMECHANIST

Back in 1998, David Leadbetter invited me to his academy headquarters in Florida to help him better understand the motion of the body during the golf swing. His knowledge of swing mechanics and my knowledge of applied biomechanics led to some terrific discussions about the complex actions of the musculoskeletal system in playing golf. Since that first meeting we've gone on to form a research partnership, studying the swings of more than four thousand golfers in the hopes of learning all we can about what the body needs to do to perform an effective and repeatable swing. David concluded from all this data that there had to be an easier way to swing the club than what was traditionally being taught. The prototypical golf swing you see week after week on the professional tours is effective in hitting good shots. But as anyone knows who has ever played this game regularly, it's difficult to master. That's why David developed the A Swing. He took our extensive research and created an alternative way to swing the club that makes it much easier to repeatedly hit good shots without having to practice for years and years.

I can say this because I put the A Swing under the microscope. David asked me to completely evaluate its motion from a scientific standpoint and compare the results to similar testing of the more traditional approach to swinging the club. Think of the powerful, dynamic, yet tough-to-copy swings of tour pros such as Justin Rose, Rory McIlroy, or Michelle Wie. For the A Swing to be worthwhile, he insisted it hold up to a high level of scrutiny—and it did. What my tests proved was that while tour pros, as a result of their talent, skill level, and endless hours of practice, do a wonderful job most of the time of repeatedly delivering the club squarely at speed into the ball with the more traditional approach, the A Swing if used by a similar athlete requires far less energy and motion to achieve comparable results. My data is provided at the end of this chapter.

There are many keys to repeatedly hitting good shots, including a player's natural athletic ability and mental focus, the equipment used, and any physical limitations he or she might have to overcome. But from a biomechanics standpoint, hitting good shots is all about controlling the kinetic energy of the club through the movement of the body. The body needs to be stable, in balance, and its motions need to be fluid and coordinated. My tests concluded that the A Swing allows golfers to achieve these requirements more easily than the traditional method.

The big thing I noticed when studying the A Swing was that it aided golfers blend, or as David terms it, synchronize, the pivot of their bodies with the swinging of the arms and club. In swinging the club, this is far and away the area where most amateurs go wrong. For example, the best golfers start the sequence of movement on the downswing with the lower body. Their feet leverage the turf, and then their hips rotate toward the target. Then they uncoil their torso, and their arms drag the clubhead through the impact zone, imparting tremendous energy into the ball. When amateurs swing, often a reverse sequence of movement occurs. The arms and club start the downswing, followed by the trunk and so on. This leads to poor contact. When I studied amateurs using the A Swing, I was so impressed with the improvement in their sequencing and synchronization. It was as if they had been doing it right for years.

Perhaps the best attribute of the A Swing is its efficiency. It helps golfers get to the top of the backswing—and poised for a good downswing—with the least wasted motion. It does this without losing the potential to build energy and create a powerful hit. My testing proved it requires less energy and movement to produce a shot of similar distance to one hit using a conventional swing. Think of how consistency will improve simply because the rotation of the body and the swinging of the arms and club are simpler and require less effort.

When you consider all of this, you can see why David and I are so excited about the potential the A Swing has for improving golfers of all skill levels. If you practice it with the seven-minute plan David outlines in this book, your swing will be more mechanically sound and easier to repeat. You'll have better footwork and balance. You'll be able to coil better in the backswing and to rotate more powerfully toward the target during the downswing. All of this will result in the club's moving on the correct path from inside the target line as you swing down, giving you your best chance of consistently hitting good shots.

I realize many of you only want the broad strokes and don't necessarily need to know the details of my A Swing testing. But for those of you who are curious, here is my explanation of how and why it works.

SYNOPSIS

To repeat any movement accurately, the goal is to simplify what is required. Think of a helicopter blade. It has to repeat the same movement up to five hundred times a minute flawlessly or the helicopter might crash. Knowing this, engineers designed the propeller to rotate around a fixed axis—the hub. This fixed point keeps the propeller rotation steady and on a constant path. In other words, it provides incredible consistency to its effective performance. Although the actions of the body and the arms and the club in the golf swing aren't identical to the action of a helicopter propeller, there are many similarities. I want you to visualize the body as that fixed axis (the hub), and the arms and the club as a propeller blade. Just as in the efficient movement of the blade, the A Swing reduces wasted motion and simplifies what is required

THE TRADITIONAL APPROACH   THE A SWING APPROACH

The club travels on a shorter, more direct route to reach the top of the backswing when using the A Swing.

of the body to let the arms swing the club around it and produce a solid shot time after time.

My testing of the A Swing in comparison to a collection of traditional swings showed:

- **Thirty percent less energy was needed to properly coil the upper body against a stable lower body—creating more powerful ground forces.**

- **Rotation around the lower body (fixed axis) was improved, with stronger activity in the core muscles.**

- **The club movement around the body was more constant, so the golfer had less need to make last-second compensations before impact to hit solid shots.**

- **The coordination of footwork improved. The transfer of weight through the feet during the backswing and through-swing was more symmetrical. The weight of the body was** supported in the right heel 45 percent more during the backswing and 45 percent more into the left heel just after impact. This indicates a better rotation of the hips during the downswing, which allows the club to swing on the proper path without being blocked by the body.

■ To produce a quality backswing, the hands traveled 20 percent less in distance than they did in a traditional swing. (This is one of the hallmarks of the A Swing and speaks to Steven Yellin's principle of least effort mentioned in the introduction.) Despite that the hands and the butt end of the club moved a shorter distance (creating a short arm swing), interestingly enough in some test cases the clubhead traveled up to 15 percent farther than in a traditional swing due to the loading of the wrists. This more compact, efficient backswing is easier to repeat and certainly offers potential for longer shots.

■ More elastic potential energy was created at the top of the backswing. The shoulder rotation increased by 10 percent as a result of better muscle synchronization, and the separation between the hips and shoulders increased by 25 percent from address to impact.

■ The center of gravity shifted 15 percent less, allowing the golfer to easily transition from backswing to downswing without losing balance.

■ Thirty percent less energy was used to generate the same amount of power. Even though the club was swung at approximately the same speed, the A Swing had better synchronization between the body rotation and the movement of the arms and club, creating better impact conditions and higher ball speeds.

■ The "smash factor" (the ratio between ball speed and clubhead speed) increased by 8 percent. In other words, golfers gained distance simply by striking the ball closer to the center of the clubface (the sweet spot) more consistently.

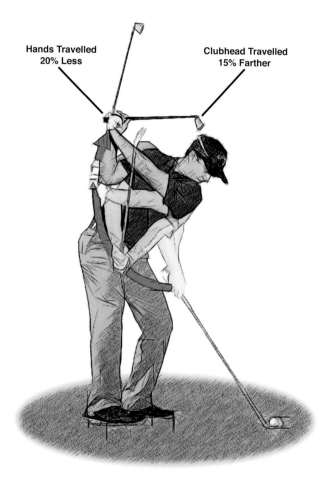

Hands Travelled
20% Less

Clubhead Travelled
15% Farther

LEFT: **On average, our test students' hands measured at the butt end of the club travelled 20% less distance than the traditional swing. The clubhead meantime, through better loading of the wrists, travelled 15% farther.**

THE BENEFITS OF THE A SWING

BELOW: **The A Swing created more elastic potential energy with less effort for average players, producing improved synchronization, better balance and improved smash factor (the ratio between ball speed and clubhead speed). Golfers gained distance by striking the ball closer to the center of the clubface as a result.**

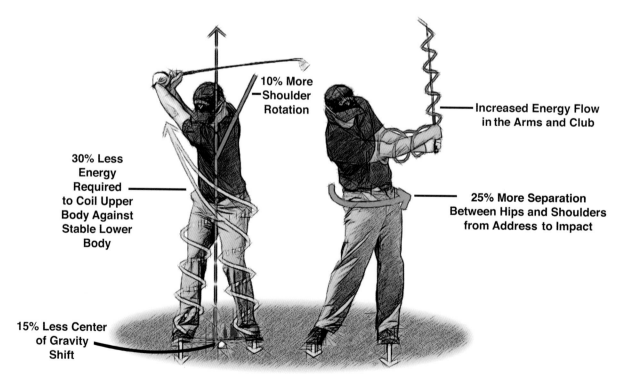

10% More
Shoulder
Rotation

Increased Energy Flow
in the Arms and Club

30% Less
Energy
Required
to Coil Upper
Body Against
Stable Lower
Body

25% More Separation
Between Hips and Shoulders
from Address to Impact

15% Less Center
of Gravity
Shift

CONCLUSIONS

- **During the initial move, less energy is needed to engage all the muscles around a stable axis. Using the deep core muscles of the abdomen creates more potential energy for the swing.**

- **It's a simpler, shorter, and more efficient motion for the hands and the club to reach the top of the swing in a good position.**

- **The club is in a better position at the top to be swung on plane during the downswing.**

- **There is more time to synchronize the downswing, which means more time to create energy to strike the ball solidly.**

- **The swing's similarity to a propeller's motion makes it easier to repeat.**

- **There is a potential to swing the club faster without losing balance, thereby resulting in longer shots.**

So in summary, the A Swing is more efficient than the standard swing, easier on the body, and simpler to learn—and it works!

Bonne chance!

When golfers are playing well—striking the ball solidly and controlling their shots—they feel their rhythm, tempo, and timing are good. Their swings feel effortless and their minds are quiet. It just feels easy, they say. But what is "it"? And why does "it" seem to come and go? Sometimes "it" can stay with you for a period. Other times, "it" appears and vanishes within the round. Excuse the play on words, but "it" is a bit of a mystery, isn't it? One thing's for sure, in a complex sequence of motion such as the golf swing, most players struggle to maintain that good feeling consistently. Even tour players at times talk about losing the feel (the "it") and swinging out of rhythm. And when "it" leaves, what was an effortless swing now feels difficult, mechanical, and requires too much thought.

CHAPTER 2

SYNCHRONIZATION —THE KEY INGREDIENT FOR GREAT GOLF

I am convinced the "it" people are referring to is synchronization. **When a golfer is in sync, the rotation of the body (component 1) and the swinging of the arms and club (component 2) are coordinated and moving in harmony, resulting in good timing and rhythm.** These two basic components must blend solidly or the golfer will not efficiently deliver good energy into the ball. Synchronization doesn't mean that the rotation of the body and the swinging of the arms and club move all together at the same speeds in the golf swing—as say synchronized swimmers would do. This would create a weak, powerless motion. What I mean by synchronization is that the two, prime components move in a coordinated sequence to produce energy, power, and, importantly, repetition. The following is somewhat of an oversimplification, but consider the swing as consisting of two circles. A portion of the smaller inner circle is the track on which your torso rotates—that's the pivot motion. Along the larger, outer circle is where the arms, hands, and club move—that's the swing movement.

The body pivots on the small, inside circle while the arms and hands swing the club on the larger, outside track.

It's paramount to coordinate and match the pivot motion with that of the swing movement—in other words, to synchronize the two circles. It's the secret to consistently hitting good shots.

The coiling and uncoiling of the body along the smaller inner circle has to be the leader in this partnership—it's the lifeblood of the golf swing, creating energy that flows through the arms and hands, and finally into the clubhead. Picture the pivot as being a small cog that drives a larger cog—the movement of the arms and club. Or as I often say, the dog (the body) has to wag the tail (the arms and club). Within these two circles, the various parts of the swing move at different speeds depending on the distance they have to travel—the longer the distance, the greater the speed. The clubhead travels on the longest route and therefore has to move faster than the hands. In turn, the hands move faster than the arms, the arms quicker than the shoulders, and the shoulders faster than the hips. This all has to happen in a coordinated sequence to produce a rhythmical swing and consistent shots. Understanding the two circles is a key step in developing good sync and plays a major part in the A Swing.

The small circle, component 1—the pivot—is, with a little understanding, relatively simple to execute. Where most golfers struggle is blending it with all the various elements of the arms-and-club aspect of the swing, i.e., the big circle, component 2—things such as the cocking and the uncocking of the wrists, the folding and the straightening of the arms, the lagging and then the squaring of the clubhead at impact, and the releasing of the club to the finish. There are a lot of moving parts. This is one of the main reasons I developed the A Swing—to make this bigger circle much simpler to do and to be more repeatable. **I would say that synchronization in the golf swing has been the essence of my teaching philosophy through the years, and all my instruction has been geared around achieving that goal.** With Michelle Wie, whom I have coached since she was thirteen, the whole approach has over the years been to get her swing in sync. With her long limbs, synchronization has always been a challenge. The more she has understood it, and the physically stronger she has become, the more in sync she has gotten. She has developed great harmony between the body and the arms, and as a result, when on, she is a superb ball-striker who has immense power and control over her shots. I believe that for the vast majority of golfers, the A Swing is the easiest way for you to get in sync.

When I teach amateurs, I'm always fascinated by how much better their pivot looks when they make the general motion without hitting a ball. I'll video them doing a drill where they mimic the body rotation during the swing with their arms folded across their chest. With just a little bit of coaching, in a short time most golfers can easily learn the pivot motion without a club. They wind their upper body against a stable lower body and load their weight onto their right side correctly as if they were making a proper backswing. Then they shift their weight onto their left side as the lower body leads a smooth- and- balanced motion toward the target as if they were making a powerful downswing. Their head remains still and they complete the movement by rotating through to a picture-perfect finish up on the right toe. The whole motion flows and looks perfectly natural. If you saw them do it, you'd think, **Wow, if they look like this when they swing a club, they'll hit good shots**.

But, alas, when I put a club in those same golfers' hands and they hit a ball, everything tends to change. The flowing practice motion disappears, and unrecognizable motion shows up in its place. Suddenly there is less coil and poor weight transfer, balance is off, the spine angle changes, the head moves all over the place, and the finish is far from graceful. The motion looks awkward. What was the cause of such a dramatic change? Well, simply, their body pivot had to react to the inefficient, complicated manner in which they swing the club. The body was no longer the leader of the motion, it was the follower—the tail is wagging the dog! Most of the faults you see with the pivot motion during the actual swing are the effect, not the cause, of a poor swing motion from the arms, hands, and club. A golfer's instinctive goal is to generate power and somehow square the clubface in time to hit the ball. Most amateurs mistakenly try to make this happen solely with their arms and hands. As a result, the natural body motion disappears and their swings often look herky-jerky and off-balance. If these same golfers could somehow improve and simplify their swing-motion component, they would have a chance to harmonize the two circles. The pivot motion would then take on the lead role and have a similar, natural look to the arms-folded-across-the-chest drill—that's the goal. I constantly remind my students that when the pivot in their actual swing looks and feels like the pivot drill without the club, then they've got it—that's when they'll play their best golf.

I have developed the A Swing to provide a simpler way for the arms, hands, and club to swing in order to facilitate a proper pivot—most swings don't allow for that to happen.

To improve your golf you don't need to have amazing flexibility or strength or have the ability to swing the club as fast as a tour pro. You simply need to learn to sync your arm swing with the pivot of the body. Sure, having flexibility and strength to make a more aggressive, coiled swing can certainly help you hit the ball farther. And having the ability to really load, cock, and uncock your wrists can create good leverage for even more power. But these are not absolute prerequisites for consistent, solid shot-making. We're all built differently with different physical attributes, and each swing has unique characteristics. So the goal is to simplify the way you swing and get the moving parts in sync. When combined properly, a good setup, solid pivot motion, and simple swing action produce consistent golf shots—more solid ones, certainly, but crucially, better bad ones, the secret to lower scoring—and that is what it is all about.

Good swings have an efficient and sequential transfer of energy. Watch a pro's downswing. The lower body moves toward the target first, or, as Jack Nicklaus says, "It unwinds from the ground up." Then the upper body uncoils and is followed by the arms and then the hands moving down toward impact. Finally the clubhead, which has lagged behind all of this action, catches up and releases its energy into the ball. It's very much like the motion when cracking a whip, and if the sequence is changed or interrupted in any way, the swing won't be nearly as efficient or effective. It takes great skill, hand-eye coordination, and timing to salvage an out-of-sync swing and still hit a decent shot. While good players often use fast-and-corrective hand action to do that—which is normally only seen when a swing is viewed in slow motion on video—most golfers don't have the ability to make that last-millisecond correction.

As a general rule, a more compact swing produces more consistent results. Logic dictates that the shorter the swing, the less the arms travel back, the easier it is to stay in sync—a lot less is going on. You'll often hear golfers say that they hit their best shots when they're only making what feels like a half swing! Problems with synchronization occur when either of the two components in the swing outraces the other. One example would be the early completion of the body's rotation in the backswing, before the arms and club have finished getting to the top, which is quite common in good players. The arms then have to "run on" independently to complete their motion to the top. Another example, which is the complete opposite, is when the arms and club get to the top before the body completes its turning and winding—seen a lot in poorer players. **The objective of the backswing is to complete rotation of the coiled upper body, and the swing of the arms and club to their destination at the top, almost in unison, just before the downswing starts.**

Synchronization problems can certainly occur on the downswing, though they are often tied into a backswing sync issue. Better players often unwind and rotate their bodies toward the target so rapidly that their arms and club lag too far behind. You might have heard some players or commentators on television refer to this as "being stuck." It means the body is too far ahead of the arms coming down—the body is early and the arms and club are late. When golfers get stuck, they have to catch up fast with their hands and arms or slow the body down in a fraction of a second to be in sync at impact—which takes a lot of talent, requires some precise timing, and is not always effective. I believe that when tour players have problems with their game, it largely results from a loss of sync, and swing changes have to be geared to getting the sync back! Meanwhile, average golfers often start the downswing almost solely with their upper bodies. Then, halfway down, the body comes to a halt but their arms and hands continue swinging. The club invariably ends up cutting across the ball on an out-to-in path, resulting in slices, pulls, you name it. Common swing faults that show up on the downswing that can be traced back to being out of sync on the backswing include:

- **Coming over the top**

- **Hitting from the top (casting)**

- **Getting stuck on the downswing**

- **Being late on it**

- **An early release**

- **Flipping the hands over through impact**

- **Collapsing the left arm through impact (the chicken wing)**

- **Spinning out**

- **Sliding**

- **Hanging back**

To fix these faults, it's essential to get to the root of the problem—poor synchronization. If you simply try to isolate and correct the fault, you might get lucky and start hitting it better for a time. But this Band-Aid, quick-fix approach generally doesn't last long. This is one of the biggest reasons I feel that the standard of golf has not improved over decades despite all the great advances in swing analysis and golf equipment. For many players the traditional approach to curing faults has been much more focused on trying to fix the effect or the symptom rather than the cause. It's like trying to fix the cracks in the walls of your house when the foundation is unstable. Those cracks will keep coming back if you don't deal with the real problem.

I realize many professional golfers, including some in the Hall of Fame, spent their entire careers sealing the odd crack in the wall—in other words, compensating in their swing for a technical flaw (you'd be surprised how many good players' swings are made up of compensations). But it took these talented athletes years of practice, persistence, and patience to perfect and repeat these compensations. They found a way to sync their swing and get to impact consistently and impart energy into the ball despite technical deficiencies. Most golfers aren't blessed with the talent or skill to compensate for their variety of swing issues. So rather than travel along that same old road of trying to fix that persistent fault, which is probably an effect anyway—it's much easier to fix the issue through understanding synchronization and finally correcting the real cause. Sync is the missing link to good golf.

That's why I believe you will find the A Swing makes sense. It gets to the heart of synchronization and improves consistency. The A Swing approach makes it so simple to blend the swinging of the club with the pivot of the body—the two circles—and that's the ultimate objective. When you correctly blend those two aspects, you can fix so many of golf's common swing faults. It allows the dog to wag the tail, which is the simplest and most effective way to play. All you have to do is simply follow my step-by-step approach—so let's get started.

The illustration below appeared in my first book, *The Golf Swing,* a revolutionary bestseller, published in 1990. The theory attached to it has been the basis of my own, and my academy instructors', teaching philosophy through the years and has stood the test of time. The picture illustrates when a dog wags its tail, or, as it relates to the golf swing, when the club moves as a result of the body motion. This fundamental principle is very much a part of the A Swing. Wag lives! Woof!

When building any solid structure, you need to have a good foundation. In golf terms, it's referred to as the setup, or address position, and consists of four things: (1) the grip; (2) posture and arm look; (3) alignment; and (4) ball position in relation to the stance. The swing is a sequential movement, and it all starts with the setup. Many swing faults can be traced back to a bad setup. That's a real shame, because it only takes a little awareness of how to stand correctly to the ball and the discipline to do it repeatedly, and a lot of swing issues can be resolved. A good setup is definitely a prerequisite for making the A Swing. This is the one area that everybody should be able to consistently repeat and master.

THE A SWING FOUNDATION

COMMON FAULTS

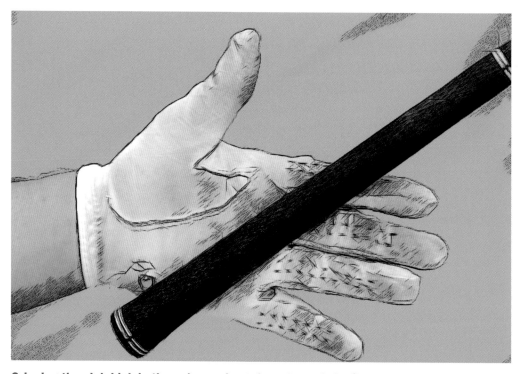

Gripping the club high in the palm, and not down toward the fingers, creates tension and unnecessary wear and tear on the heel pad of the glove.

1.   **GRIPPING THE CLUB IN THE PALM OF THE LEFT HAND. I believe this is the single biggest fault in golf. In my estimation, probably at least 80 percent of golfers have this problem. Wherever I go in the world, it's an epidemic. Many right-handed players grip the club high in the palm of their left hand as opposed to down toward the fingers. A telltale sign you're gripping the club incorrectly is wear and tear on the heel pad of your golf glove, or in extreme cases a hole is formed. This comes from friction on the glove, as the club shifts around in the palm.**

Most golfers grab hold of the club and position it in the palm simply because they don't know any better, and it feels secure this way. It's a case where what feels natural is wrong! Also, for a lot of golfers the actual grip of the club is the wrong size for them—it's either too thick or too thin, forcing the club into the palm (I recommend having the thickness checked by your pro or a club-fitter). Whatever the reason, palming the grip creates tremendous tension, and the hands and the arms get overly active early in the backswing. The palmy grip also

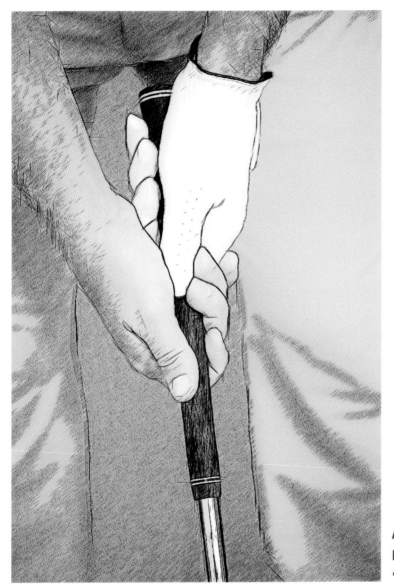

A typical bad grip—A "weak"
left-hand position and a
"strong" right-hand position.

restricts the natural cocking action of the left wrist—an important power factor in the swing. A common look we see associated with this palmy grip is termed a *weak* left hand, meaning the hand is positioned too far around to the left side of the club's handle, where you might see just one knuckle as opposed to two or three. Meanwhile, the right hand tends to get into a *strong*, grabby position. It's almost rolled underneath the handle. This poor grip is a bad way to start the swing and leads to a whole host of faults.

Poor posture restricts the body from moving correctly.

Tension in the arms at address prevents a free-flowing swing.

2. **HUNCHING OVER AT ADDRESS AND HOLDING THE CLUB WITH TENSE ARMS.** Setting up with poor or sloppy posture—which includes a rounded spine, locked or overly bent knees, a tucked head—and holding the club with tension in the arms prevent the body from moving correctly during the swing. It's essential to set up in a way that you can swing the club freely—on a consistent track—while staying in balance. Tight arms are one of the leading causes of poor rhythm and tempo. The hands and arms have to be relaxed at the start so that they don't dominate the initial phase of the swing. The problem with tension is that it reduces the ability of the body to transfer energy down through the arms and hands and into the club, resulting in poor contact.

A common problem with alignment—golfers align their feet to the target, and forget about the upper body.

3. MISALIGNING YOUR BODY IN RELATION TO THE TARGET. Aiming can be difficult, because unlike in golf, say, in archery, where you set your body and eyes on the target line behind the arrow, you have to stand perpendicular to your target and to the side of your golf ball. Often golfers just pay attention to the position of their feet and forget how their hips and shoulders should be aligned in relation to the target. Setting the upper body correctly is crucial. Many wayward shots can be traced back to poor alignment of the shoulders and/or hips.

Ball position too far forward in the stance, often seen with slicers.

Ball position too far back in the stance, often seen with hookers of the ball.

4. ADDRESSING THE BALL TOO FAR FORWARD OR TOO FAR BACK IN THE STANCE.
Ball-position issues, apart from general ignorance, tend to result from a player's swing tendencies. For example, slicers who swing on a path that cuts across the target line from out-to-in will generally address the ball way forward in their stance to compensate. A player who swings severely in-to-out and hooks the ball will tend to play it too far back in the stance. Ball-position problems can occur with every club in the bag. For instance, many golfers are unaware that they address the ball in the same position with their driver as they do with an iron, which creates a problem. Or, just as common is the golfer having the ball way forward in the stance with an iron in an attempt to get the ball up in the air. As I will explain later, the length of the club dictates the ball position.

Now that you are aware of some of the common faults at address that could hurt your ability to strike the ball, here's how to build a great foundation for the A Swing.

THE GRIP

I recommend gripping the club in a way that's different from the standard approach, but it's an integral part of the whole A Swing and is quite natural. It might feel strange at first, but it's designed to get your hands and wrists working correctly. As the late golf legend Ben Hogan once said, "Good golf begins with a good grip." Interpretations of what a good grip is vary. But in our testing of the A Swing, I've found the grip I'm about to teach you is important to achieve the final goal—generating maximum clubhead speed and squaring the face of the club at impact so you can routinely hit the ball long and straight.

Because of the importance of the grip in the A Swing, and because it is different from what is considered traditional, I want to initially discuss the way both hands should look on the club. I will then take you through exactly how to get your hands in the desired position.

The hand positions mirror each other—the "prayer grip."

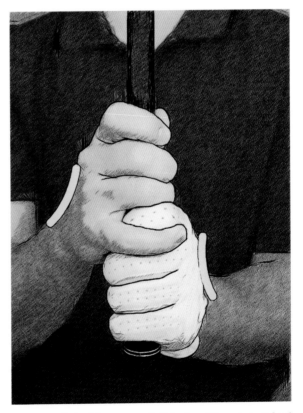

The completed "prayer grip" look with symmetrical "cups."

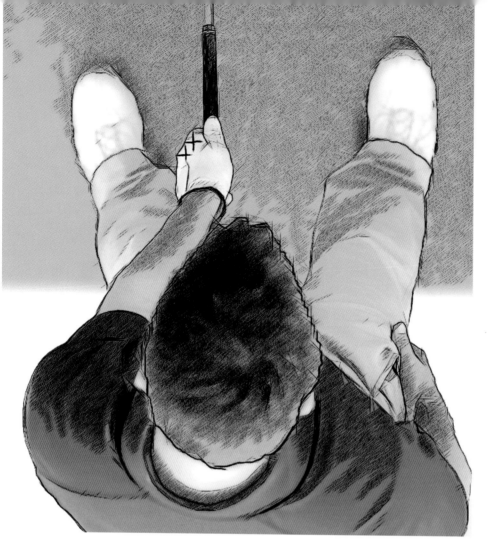

When you look down, two to three knuckles should be seen on the left hand.

The grip is what I would describe as a natural, neutral-hand position—the left hand mirrors the right. I call it the prayer grip because when you hold your hands up in front of you, the angles, or cups, at the base of the right and left wrists are symmetrical as they would be if your hands were together in a praying position.

For right-handed golfers, the position of the left hand is termed *strong* in golfing terminology (around to the right on the club). When you look down at your left hand as you address the ball, you should see two to three knuckles and the forefinger in line with your right eye.

Conversely, the right hand is termed *weak* (rotated over to the left side of the golf shaft). The right forefinger should be in line with your left eye. (*Strong* and *weak* have nothing to do with how much pressure you are applying or if the grip is tight or loose.)

Gripping the club in this symmetrical manner, which many of the test students said quickly felt comfortable, gives you a softness in the wrists that allows them to set and load correctly. It also gives the hands the ability to square and release the clubhead through the impact zone.

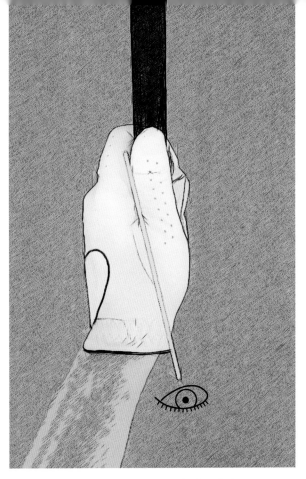

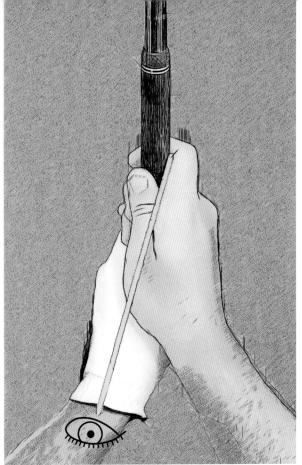

The left forefinger is in line with the right eye.

The right forefinger is in line with the left eye.

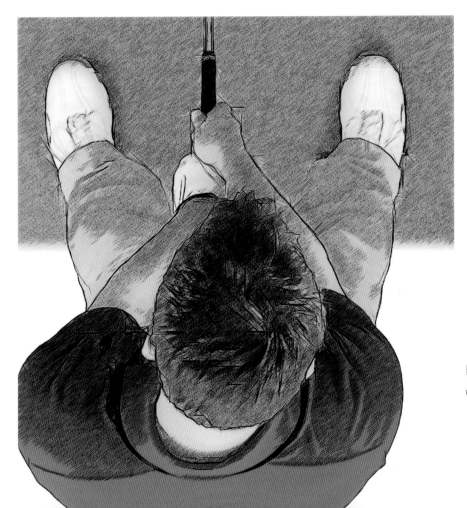

Looking down at the completed grip.

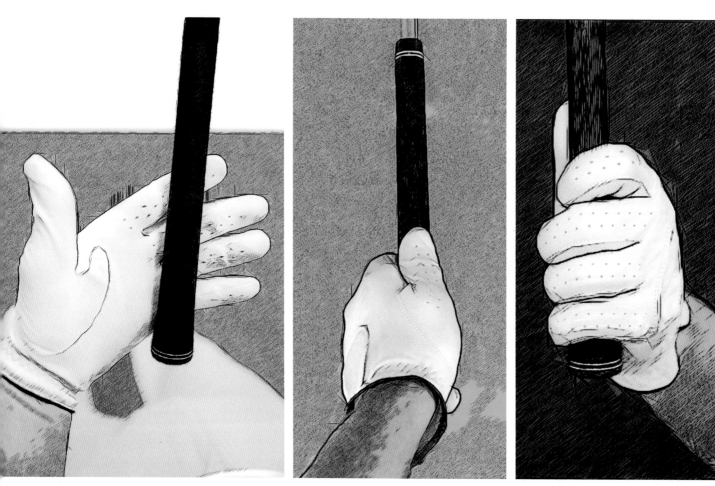

1. Lay the handle of the club across the fingers and palm.

2. The thumb and forefinger together form an important link.

3. The first knuckle on the left forefinger juts out as if resting on a trigger.

So now that you understand what the grip should look like, here's the process you need to go through to get your A Swing grip. Start with the left hand.

Grip the club so that the handle lies diagonally across the lower part of the palm and the fingers. The shaft should rest against the crook of the forefinger. When you close the hand on the grip, the left thumb touches the first knuckle of the forefinger (an important link in a solid grip) and sits fairly straight down the shaft. The first knuckle of the left forefinger juts out a touch, as if it were resting on a trigger.

The palm of the right hand rests on top of the left thumb.

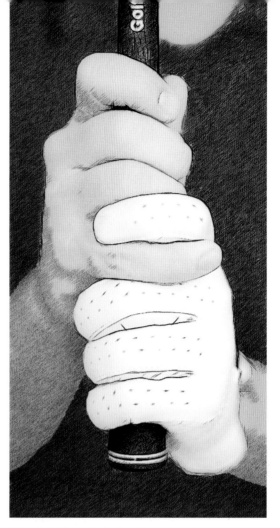

The right hand's index finger rests on a trigger.

Now for the right hand. The lifeline must sit on top of the left thumb like a tongue-and-groove joint. Make sure the base of the palm is covering the left thumb, with both your thumbs in an almost parallel position and stacked on top of each other. Wrap the hand around the grip and let the right index finger separate itself slightly from the middle finger as if it were also resting on a trigger.

Once you've got the hands in the correct positions, you have to choose a way to link them together so they work as a unit. The three choices are a matter of personal preference. First there is the overlapping Vardon style, made popular in the early part of the twentieth century by the great Harry Vardon. When using this grip, the pinkie finger of the right hand rests on top of the crease between the middle and index fingers of the left hand. The golfer shown in this book uses this grip, as do the majority of pros. Another grip is termed the baseball grip, with the right hand simply placed below the left. This method can be helpful for golfers with small or weak hands, those who suffer from arthritis, or anyone trying to generate more clubhead speed. The third option is the interlocking style, used by Jack Nicklaus and Tiger Woods. In this grip, the pinkie of the right hand and the index finger of the left hand are coupled.

Although all three will work well with the A Swing, I prefer the interlocking method. I like how it enables the hands to sit softly on the club, and I think it makes the prayer grip feel the most comfortable. **The key to this grip is that the two linked fingers—the pinkie and index—are relaxed and protruding slightly and not resting fully on the club, thus reducing pressure in the middle of the grip.** The problem with most interlocking grips is that golfers who use them tend to jam their pinkie and index fingers too far in, squeezing them together, which creates far too much tension. Removing the tension from these two fingers allows the wrists to set easily.

In overall grip pressure, you want to sense a little extra on the club with the last two fingers of the left hand, and the thumb and forefinger of the right hand, but with virtually no pressure in the middle of the grip. These pressure patterns help you maintain control of the club; aid in cocking and loading the wrists on the backswing for more leverage; and help retain wrist cock (lag) well into the downswing, which adds more power to your shots.

1. The overlapping grip   2. The baseball grip   3. The interlocking grip

Regardless of the style you use, you want your grip pressure overall to feel light, certainly not loose, but only firm enough so that if you were to raise the club off the ground, you would sense the weight of it in your hands. If you could put a number on overall grip pressure—10 being the tightest—your goal is to have a 3 or a 4. Employing this soft grip keeps the tension out of your arms and shoulders, which is so important for a fluid swing.

The A Swing grip allows the hands and wrists to work correctly in the swing while maintaining control and stability of the club.

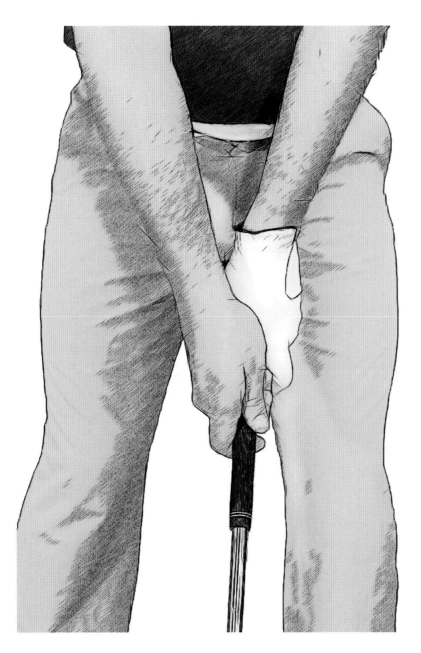

**The completed
A Swing grip**

GRIP NUGGETS

- Grip the club with a strong left-hand position and weak right-hand position (prayer look).

- Lay the club diagonally across the lower palm and fingers of the left hand.

- Keep overall grip pressure light (about 3 or 4 out of 10).

POSTURE AND ARM LOOK

Standing in an athletic, yet relaxed, posture at address will go a long way toward developing a powerful and repeatable swing. If your body angles are sharp and concise, you'll have a much better chance of maintaining your balance as you wind and unwind your body around a stable axis. It all starts with a solid base formed by your feet, knees, and thighs to support the rotating trunk. Just as important as good posture is the positioning of your arms at address. If your posture is poor, it will be difficult to position your arms correctly. And vice versa.

To ensure both are good, go through this routine (it's helpful to check it in a mirror): Using the prayer grip, stand tall holding a 6-iron in front of you so the shaft points straight up. With your arms relaxed, pull the shoulder blades down, elevate the sternum, and let the elbows rest on your rib cage. With your legs straight and your feet slightly flared and set with the distance between the big toes about shoulder width, bend from the hip joints so your upper body tilts forward and your tailbone moves backward until your butt is behind your heels. Keep the club elevated until you feel a tightening sensation in your hamstrings and calves. In this position, you will feel pressure going down through the middle of your feet, with your body weight evenly distributed.

Now soften and slightly flex your knees (but don't overly bend them) and bump your left hip up and to the left slightly (the left hip should be about a half inch to one inch higher than the right). This will tilt your spine to the right, or slightly away from the target. This is particularly important to do when swinging a driver, so check your shirt buttons in a mirror and make sure that they are leaning to the right. The final step is to lower and sole the club until it's resting lightly on the ground. Feel the arms relaxed and the elbows slightly bowed. Once the club is grounded, you should feel a combination of being relaxed and tension-free with your upper body, yet solid and athletic with your lower body.

A way to ensure that you are standing the correct distance from the ball, with every club, is that when you are in your completed address position, check that your upper arms are lying lightly on your chest. If you have no connection with your arms at all, you're too far from the ball. If your elbows rest on your chest, then you're too close.

Get into your address posture starting from this position.

Bend from the hip joints, and let your tailbone move backward.

Relaxed arms at address

Sole the club and slightly flex the knees.

The left hip sits higher than the right—the spine tilts away from the target.

Clapping the hands gives the correct arm look.

Okay, now you have to get the right look and feel with the arms. Here's a simple drill: In front of a mirror, assume the address position without a club. Let your arms hang loosely in front of you with your upper arms resting on the chest and the hands about six inches apart. Now clap your hands together. Sense the softness of the arms and notice the shape after clapping—both elbows slightly bowed. Try to re-create this sensation when you take your address with a club.

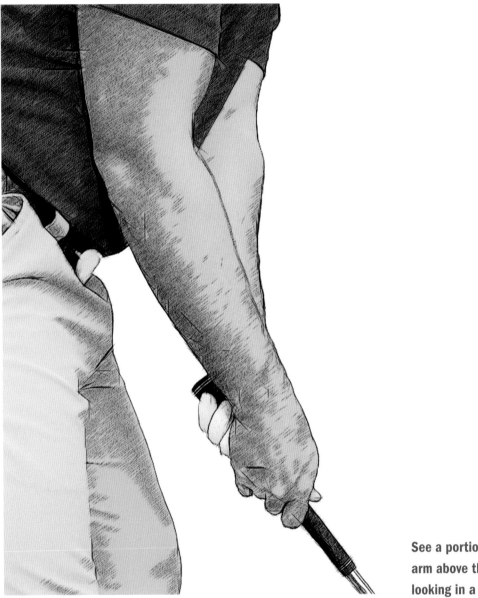

See a portion of your left arm above the right when looking in a mirror.

There's one final thing to do. Again with the aid of a mirror, grab a club and get back into your address position as if you're swinging away from your reflection. When you look back over your right shoulder at the mirror, relax and lower your right arm so you see a portion of your left arm above it. This is particularly important to check when adopting the prayer grip, as it indicates that your shoulders are properly aligned parallel to the target line.

THE **A** SWING

POSTURE AND ARM LOOK NUGGETS

- Bend from the hips.

- Pull the shoulder blades down but keep the sternum up.

- Keep the arms tension free.

ALIGNMENT

As I mentioned earlier, aiming the body and club correctly can be a challenge because you're standing to the side of the ball and not directly on your target line as you would be if you were shooting an arrow with a bow, or firing a rifle. **The key for consistent aiming is to first align the clubface to the target and** then **set your body so it's on a parallel line left of where the clubface is pointing.** The classic way to describe this is to imagine you were standing on railway tracks—your clubface resting on one track and your body standing on the other.

If you can re-create this imagery, getting everything above your feet (knees, hips, shoulders, and even your eyes) matching and set parallel left of your target line, you're properly aligned.

The clubface aims at the target on one rail—your body parallel on the other.

A closed-feet position is recommended for the A Swing.

Having said this, though, I would like you to make this little adjustment. In developing the A Swing, I've found significant benefit in adjusting your toe line two or three inches so the feet (feet only) are aimed in a slightly closed position right of your target. It is also good to point out that of all the alignment components, the feet are the least important in affecting the swing. Many of the great players set up this way, including Ben Hogan, Sam Snead, and Bobby Jones. I'll explain the benefits of the closed-feet stance in the following chapters, but in the meantime, here is how you do it. Once you have established a square position with your body, parallel to the left of your target—including the feet—move your right foot away from the target line and your left foot forward toward it so that the tip of your right shoe lines up approximately with the front of the laces of your left shoe. Always set up square initially, then work into this closed position with your feet. All the other alignment factors—knees, hips, shoulders, eyes—must remain unaltered.

ALIGNMENT NUGGETS

- Align the clubface at the target *first*.

- Set the eyes, shoulders, hips, and knees parallel and left of that target line.

- Adjust the feet so the toe line is pointing slightly right of the target line.

BALL POSITION

People have different theories about where the ball should be positioned within the stance. Some say—which is the old theory—that the ball should be aligned with the left heel when using a driver, then more progressively back in the stance as the club used gets shorter. Another approach is to keep the ball in one spot, close to the left heel, and then slightly narrow your stance as the club gets shorter.

I have found what works best with the A Swing is to think about the ball being addressed in one of three locations. With your irons, your goal is to swing down to impact with a descend-

Ball positioned close to the middle of the stance for the irons to accommodate a downward strike.

Ball positioned forward in the stance with the driver for a sweeping upward strike.

Ball positioned between the iron and the driver for hybrids and fairway woods.

ing angle and take a divot in front of the ball. To achieve this, address the ball in the middle or just forward of the middle of your stance (feet closer together for short irons). When using a driver, your goal is to sweep the ball off the tee by hitting slightly up on it after the clubhead passes the bottom of the swing arc. For this to happen, play the ball closer to your front foot. Finally, when using a fairway wood or hybrid, the ball should be struck near the bottom of the swing arc. The angle of the clubhead into the ball must be neither too downward nor upward— although many good fairway-wood players do take a tiny divot after impact. The ball position here is roughly halfway between the driver and iron locations (between the left heel and the center of your stance).

You can check the ball's location when practicing by placing two alignment rods (see "The A Swing Training Aids" at the end of the book) or golf shafts on the ground. Place one parallel to your target line and the other one perpendicular to it between your feet (indicating the ball's position). This facet of setup is fairly easy to keep constant as long as you check it periodically. Finally, just to reiterate, the width of your stance gets fractionally narrower as the club gets shorter. The width of the stance also has a feel aspect: to get solidly balanced, take into account wind, how level the lie is, etc. Generally speaking, the stance needs to be fairly wide with the driver, where you need good balance to make an aggressive swing and the lower body plays a bigger role, but it's fairly narrow when you're using a short iron.

BALL POSITION NUGGETS

- Address the ball in one of three locations: centered for irons, off the front heel for a driver, and halfway between those two points for a fairway wood or hybrid.

- Check the ball position in relation to your stance with an alignment rod.

CONCLUSION FOR THE A SWING FOUNDATION

You might find that working on building a better foundation is pretty boring, but it's hard to overemphasize how important it is for what happens next in the swing. It's the start of the chain. Tour pros are constantly checking their foundation because they know that even a slight alteration to it can create problems in the swing. They realize the foundation forms the basis for consistency in their game, and it is the easiest part of the equation to perfect because it takes place before the swing starts. It takes just a little bit of discipline to develop and maintain a good foundation. I suggest checking yours in a mirror periodically. Trust me, if you worked on it and did nothing else, you would play better. One can gauge the quality of a player simply by looking at how well he or she sets up to the ball. To that point, it's the first drill in my seven-minute practice plan.

The pivot motion of the body is the lifeblood of the golf swing. It is the hub of the swing, the power source. To understand the swing and to strike the ball solidly, it's important to be aware of how the pivot motion works—how the body winds up on the backswing creating power, then unwinds on the downswing unleashing that power. The body creates the energy and in a sequential action passes it on to the arms, hands, and club, which in turn deliver it into the ball. So mastering the pivot motion is essential in developing your A Swing.

CHAPTER 4

THE A SWING PIVOT MOTION

COMMON FAULTS

Overturning of the hips
and shoulders is a sign you
haven't coiled properly.

1. **A LACK OF COILING DURING THE BACKSWING. If you do not wind up the big back muscles against some resistance with the lower body on the backswing, this lack of coil will create an overuse of the arms and upper body on the downswing—affecting distance and accuracy. A big turn of the hips and shoulders without any coil happens when a golfer focuses on the overused word *turn*. Coiling is much more important than turning. A big turn does not necessarily create more coil! Good coiling on the backswing leads to the proper sequencing on the way down, where the lower body leads and the upper body follows—the sequence of all good ball-strikers.**

A change of spine
angle affects
consistency.

2. A CHANGE OF THE SPINE ANGLE DURING THE SWING. Any significant changes in
the spine angle as you rotate your trunk during the backswing or downswing (which creates visibly excessive head movement) produces problems with one's ball-striking. This
fault occurs for a number of reasons, starting with bad posture. Elevating or lowering
the spine during the swing results in poor balance, overuse of the hands and arms, and
general inconsistency. To have a repeatable swing, it is vital for the forward bend of the
spine created at address to remain constant up to the point of impact—certainly with
an iron (the driver, as we will discuss, is slightly different).

Swaying during the backswing and downswing

3. **POOR WEIGHT TRANSFER.** The first problem in poor weight transfer is when a golfer sways away from the target during the backswing and then sways toward it during the downswing. The second is when a golfer reverse-pivots—instead of the weight's moving correctly back to the right side, and then on to the left, it does the opposite! With the sway, golfers have too much lateral weight shift in their swings. They either sway their body weight to the outside of their back foot on the backswing, or they excessively sway or slide their bodies forward laterally on the downswing—or they do both. Basically, not enough rotary motion occurs in the torso, which creates more of a circular weight movement as opposed to a linear one. This sway action of the body is often accompanied by the head's moving too much from side to side, which makes it even more difficult to hit solid shots.

The reverse pivot—the weight stays on the left on the backswing, and moves to the right on the downswing.

With the reverse pivot, a lot of weight remains on the left side of the body at the top of the swing and then, as a counteraction, shifts back to the right on the downswing. This problem often stems from exaggeratedly trying to keep the head still or down—a common piece of bad advice espoused through the decades that restricts proper, fluid weight movement. The correct transfer of weight is essential, especially with longer shots, to provide momentum and power.

An example of lower-body instability—locked right leg—active left foot and knee.

4. **UNSTABLE LOWER BODY. This is caused either by overly active movement of the feet and ankles or too much bending/locking or collapsing of the knees during either the backswing or the downswing. Without stability and solid grounding, it's difficult to make a consistently good swing. The feet and lower body provide the base for good balance, power, and control.**

DEVELOPING THE PIVOT

To make learning the A Swing pivot clearer, I'm going to break it down into three sections. Section one is the backswing motion. Section two is the transition from the backswing into the downswing motion. Section three is the downswing, follow-through, and finish motion. Once you've learned and practiced the movements individually in each section, you'll blend them together into one smooth, continuous action.

To start, position your body in the athletic posture outlined in the previous chapter and give yourself a hug by resting your arms across your belly or core (you don't need a club for this drill). Your hands should be touching the opposite sides of the body. As I briefly mentioned in the last chapter, you should also be standing with your feet approximately shoulder-width apart and in a closed stance, aligned to the right of an imaginary target. Having your right foot pulled back so its toes are in line with the front of the shoelaces on the left foot aids the pivot motion. First, it helps to fully wind you up during the backswing as it frees up your right hip to move behind you. Second, it encourages the hips to shift slightly to the right of the target at the start of the downswing (an important part of the transition as you will see, as opposed to the hips rotating and opening toward the target too soon, a common fault referred to as spinning out). Once you set your feet correctly, you're in position to work through the three sections of the pivot.

Start the pivot drill from this position.

SECTION ONE OF THE PIVOT

The spiral winding of the spine

Use your belly to start the pivot.

The right side stretches up and the left side lowers—a spiraling rotation.

I'm going to emphasize the early part of the pivot. The feeling you want is that your belly initiates the movement by using the all-important core muscles. You will sense this as a result of your hands' resting on your midsection at address. It's important that your belly is moving, as opposed to the hips just turning. This creates more coiling right from the outset. The major movement of the backswing is initiated from deep in your core, and as the spine winds, the energy spirals up through the torso just like wringing out a wet towel. In conjunction with the core activity, let the left shoulder move down and the right shoulder move up. This tilting action of the shoulders works in conjunction with the right hip hiking upward and the left hip going down. This stretching up of the right side and lowering of the left gets the shoulders turning on the proper plane and maximizes the coiling of the big back muscles against a stable lower body as you complete the backswing.

Although there is obviously a turning motion in the swing, remember to think of this as more of a coiling, winding, and spiraling process instead of just turning. These words have a much more powerful connotation. **Remember you can turn without coil, but you cannot coil without turn.** Here is the sequence of the first section of the pivot motion:

- **The belly or core initiates the movement.**

- **Move the left shoulder and hip down, the right shoulder and hip up, the left knee inward.**

- **Wind the chest and the big back muscles on top of the right leg.**

- **Sense pressure building in the right heel, knee, and quadriceps muscles.**

- **Wind the torso fully so the right side of the body feels elevated and the left side feels low—a spiral rotation.**

- **Sense both feet are screwed into the ground and are providing solid stability.**

- **Keep the head fairly centered and stationary (although the chin can rotate).**

- **Wind and rotate the upper body about twice the amount of the lower body. For example, the shoulders should rotate roughly ninety degrees while the hips rotate about forty-five degrees (this amount varies, depending on flexibility).**

The upper back is angled away from the vertical at the top.

Check yourself in a mirror when you have completed this first section of the pivot. To fully load into your right side with a full rotation of the torso, your upper back should be angled away from the vertical—especially with the longer clubs.

Section one of the pivot is all about what moves what. Certainly the shoulders and the hips turn. But in reality, what's moving internally (your core muscles) is key to getting started correctly. Sections two and three of the pivot are a sequential reaction to section one. So it's vital to get a feel for the first part so the rest of the pivot will happen automatically in sequence.

SECTION TWO OF THE PIVOT

A good transition from backswing to downswing is a trait common to all good players. The proper movement, especially when viewed in slow motion, is dynamic and crucial to good ball-striking. **For a split second, you'll be moving in two directions at once. The lower body (hips and knees) will be moving toward the target, while the upper body (chest and shoulders), arms, and club are still going back.** This is why in many good swings there appears to be a pause at the top as this action takes place. This change of direction is an extremely powerful move and significantly increases the torque on the body. As you learned in section one of the pivot, your shoulders will wind about twice the amount that the hips do—let's use the example of ninety degrees versus forty-five degrees, which is a differential of forty-

Showing the differential between shoulder rotation and hip rotation —45°

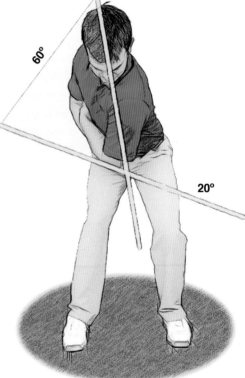

If the lower body begins the downswing while the upper body is still completing the backswing, the differential between shoulder and hip rotation will increase—60° compared to 45°. This is a powerful move. (Note: There will be a slight unwinding of the shoulders from say 90° to 80° in the transition.)

five degrees. If the transition is dynamic, the differential between the shoulders and hips increases even more, perhaps another fifteen or twenty degrees, say to sixty degrees, because of this powerful change of direction. If you are able to start your lower body moving toward the target while your upper body is still going back, you'll be absolutely amazed at the strike you put on the ball. This whole action has to be smooth—don't rush it—as it's a key part of synchronization. It is just a the batter in baseball stepping into the pitch with his lower body as his upper body is still winding up and taking the bat back. It provides extra stretch to an imaginary rubber band before it snaps back.

It takes patience and some practice to develop the coordination to make this dynamic transition. This can be achieved by doing the pivot drill regularly. Initially when learning it, you will stop at the top when doing the pivot exercise and then start the forward movement. But eventually you will blend the backswing and downswing together, so part of you will start down while the rest is still going back. If you lack flexibility and can't create a huge differential between the coiling of your shoulders and your hips, that's okay—you can still increase whatever differential you have as you change direction. That's the key thing in the transition.

Here is the sequence of motion:

- **At the top of the swing, feel coiled and wound with pressure in your right heel. (When you start doing the three sections of the pivot drill without pausing, you'll still be winding and spiraling your upper body as your lower body starts the movement forward.)**

- **Start the movement with the lower body by letting your left hip glide laterally forward and to the right of the target.**

- **Sense your back faces the target with your hips and shoulders pointing to the right.**

- **Feel pressure building on the front and inside of your left foot, while keeping some pressure in your right heel as the weight starts to transfer off the right leg. This is termed being grounded, because your right foot stays flat on the ground at this point.**

- **Allow your spine and your head to drift slightly toward the target as your body weight shifts onto your left side.**

- **Sense that the left side of your body, from the shoulder down to the knee, feels low and compressed.**

Keep rehearsing section two, and remember that this transition is a short movement—the key is to be aware of the pressure in your feet as you do it, both in the right heel and the front of the left foot.

SECTION THREE OF THE PIVOT

The final piece of the pivot motion is the full unwinding of the body toward the target. This happens in a flash. So get to the transition point and follow this guideline:

- **Clear your hips out of the way and allow the pressure on the front of the left foot to move back toward the heel.**

- **Roll the right foot over so the pressure is now toward the front and inside portion of the foot.**

The left leg straightens and the left side stretches upward.

- **Sense a straightening of the left leg as the left side of the body (pelvis, hip, and shoulders) clears and stretches upward—the opposite of what takes place in the backswing.**

The spine angle is maintained through impact; the hips and shoulders open up as the right shoulder moves down and forward.

■ While maintaining the spine angle created at address, continue to open up your hips and clear the left shoulder out of the way while the right shoulder moves down and forward. This is the point where the right side really gets into the act. In the impact area, the hips to a greater extent and the shoulders are pointed to the left, or open to the target, well past the square position they started in at address.

A completed, well-balanced pivot

■ **Complete the unwinding motion of the body with the right shoulder being the closest thing to the target.**

Feel like you could walk toward the target from this finish position.

■ At the finish, hold your balance, stand tall with the knees touching, up on the right toe, and the hips fully rotated around. You should feel as if you could without a lot of effort walk forward toward the target from this position.

The complete pivot motion

Breaking this motion up into three sections and rehearsing them, with the aid of the drawings, will quickly develop your awareness for a perfect pivot. Once you feel comfortable doing each of the sections, link them together into one continuous, fluid motion and practice until it becomes instinctive. (Suggestion: doing it with your eyes closed speeds up the learning curve.) With no arms or club to get in the way, and no ball to hit, it makes learning the motion quite simple. Looking at your pivot, an observer would see a well-sequenced movement where you coil on the backswing, unload with the lower body on the downswing, and finish in balance—all the attributes of a good swing.

I've made a few references to how physical limitations might influence your ability to make a full pivot. The A Swing works even with a fairly limited pivot. I don't want you to worry that you're not strong enough or flexible enough to do it perfectly (although the exercises in chapter 7 can help you make improvements in these areas). The A Swing is designed for golfers of all physical abilities and has a great range of tolerance. It's not how big of a movement you make—it's just that the movement you do make must be balanced, coiled, and rhythmical.

I'm often asked if the left heel can come off the ground when making the backswing pivot. Ideally it should stay planted, as it is one less move to worry about. However, if you do lack some flexibility or feel that your body motion does not provide enough power to get the club accelerating and you are lacking distance, then do this: raise the left heel off the ground a little on the backswing while maintaining stability in your left knee—you don't want it to be wobbly. This way, your lower body will still provide the resistance to wind your upper body against. As you swing down, replant the left heel so you feel pressure moving into the front of the foot before it goes back to the heel. This move will help provide you with extra energy to get that clubhead really moving.

The pivot is the basis of the swing, and when you combine it with what you learn in the next chapter, you will be surprised at how little effort it takes to hit a solid shot. One of the benefits of working on this pivot motion is that, over time, it will naturally increase your flexibility, rotational speed, and endurance. It's a mini exercise program in itself. In fact, it appears as one of the six exercises in the practice plan in chapter 7.

PIVOT MOTION FEELS

I just covered a lot of ground in describing how to pivot correctly, but in my experience it does not take that long for a golfer to develop a technically sound body motion. To further enhance the feel for the pivot motion, here are some biomechanical images and drills.

In the pivot motion, sense the hips as moving in a figure-eight like motion, feeling an increase in pressure from the ground into to the right heel then, into the front of the left foot, and finally around to the left heel.

- **To blend the three sections into one, *sense the hips moving in a figure-eight motion.* The right hip goes up and behind you during the backswing portion of the pivot; the left hip moves to the right of the target as you start the transition; the left hip moves up and clears to the left during the downswing, and the right hip then follows it into the finish position. Linked with this image is the way you build up pressure down into the ground through the right heel on the backswing, moving on to the front of the left foot in the transition, and then back around to the left heel at the finish.**

  J. J. Rivet discovered this movement pattern many years ago, and it is key for stability and power in the golf swing. He calls it foot grounding. Many teachers have now adopted this philosophy for the proper lower-body motion.

To sense the backswing pivot, allow the arms to slide up and down your thighs in a pistonlike motion.

■ To sense the proper movement pattern of the shoulders, the upward stretching of the right side and the winding of the core in a spiraling fashion during the backswing phase of the pivot motion, do this exercise: Get into your address posture and let your arms hang down by your sides with your hands resting on your thighs. Your right arm should hang lower than the left, so your spine is tilted to the right as it would appear at address. Using an up-and-down, pistonlike motion, with stable knees and solid feet, allow your left hand to slide down your thigh while your right hand slides up on the opposite leg. You will get the sensation of your left side tilting lower and your right side getting higher with an internal coiling and winding sensation starting from your midsection and spiraling upward—a sign your core muscles are working properly. Complete the winding motion to the top, where you should feel a stretch across your chest and upper back—the left knee appears lower than the right knee; the left hip lower than the right; the left shoulder considerably lower than the right. Doing this drill will enable your torso to simply react and make a similar (matching) move as you unwind and unspiral on the downswing before working to the finish.

■ To sense how to stabilize the pelvis, which keeps the spine angle (forward bend) constant up to impact, do the pivot drill with your butt against a wall. Pivot back, and then as you move into the transition phase and the left hip leads, let your right buttock slide along the wall a few inches so that the right leg stays behind the left. Feel a little pressure in the right heel and a lot of pressure down through the front of the left foot. As you continue into the downswing and follow-through phase of the pivot, let your body rotate. As this is happening, reconnect the left buttock with the wall and now feel pressure down through your left heel. This is a great drill to feel the dynamics of the pivot motion.

THE A SWING

PIVOT MOTION NUGGETS

- Initiate the movement on the backswing with your core muscles—the left shoulder moves down and the right shoulder moves up in a spiraling fashion. Feel pressure in the right heel.

- Feel pressure transfer into the front of the left foot during the pivot's transition into the downswing.

- Keep your back turned away from the target and let your hips glide laterally and slightly to the right of the target.

- Unwind your body around the left leg, feeling pressure going into the left heel.

- Think of the entire pivot motion as winding, gliding, and unwinding.

- Sense the right side of the body elevating and stretching up on the backswing, and the left side doing the same on the downswing into the finish.

- Learn each section individually, then blend them into one powerful pivot motion.

CONCLUSION FOR THE A SWING PIVOT MOTION

When you are swinging the club, ultimately your pivot action needs to look and feel like the pivot drill. **The pivot has to be the leader in the swing.** If the arms and hands are the controlling factors, in no way will the pivot look or feel the same as in the drill. **Remember the arms, hands, and club complement the pivot motion—they do not control it.** The pivot motion does more than just create the power and energy in a swing—it also controls the pace and tempo. Allowing the movement of the body to pace the speed of the arms and club aids in consistency and repetition. This is what is meant by the phrase **using the big muscles in the swing.**

By now you should have a good understanding of the pivot motion that I detailed in chapter 4. It's essential that you know how your body moves before learning how to swing the club. The pivot motion I outline is not revolutionary. The consensus among instructors, biomechanists, and physiologists is that the body should basically move this way to execute a good swing. I have always believed in building a golf swing that you develop the pivot motion *before* incorporating it with the swinging of the club—and that certainly holds true with the A Swing. I've found that learning the components separately, then blending them together in a cohesive and efficient movement, is much easier than trying to work on everything at the same time.

CHAPTER

5

THE A SWING ARMS-AND-CLUB MOVEMENT

Typically golfers catch on to the concept of a proper pivot motion pretty quickly without a ball—the body wants to move in this fashion and it looks natural. But those same golfers would probably struggle to execute the pivot correctly when it's time to hit the ball. This is because of the inefficient manner in which the club is typically swung. Instead of the body pivoting correctly, it has to react and compensate for all of the wasted motion of the arms and club during the swing. Thus the motions with and without a club look very different. This is why you see so many faulty pivot motions among amateurs. A total loss of synchronization occurs as a result. The hands and arms are incorrectly dictating the body pivot. Your goal is to make the motion of the arms and club as efficient and easy to repeat as possible, so the body is able to pivot in the way it should. The A Swing will help make that happen. It allows you to develop a simple arms-and-club movement to complement the pivot. At this stage I am describing the A Swing using an iron. With an iron, the goal is to hit the ball with a descending blow. However, no matter what club you're using, the swinging motion of the arms and club should feel identical—especially during the backswing. For example, when using a driver, the length of the club and the correct setup and ball position will help you hit up on the ball. So basically one swing motion fits all!

COMMON FAULTS

An inside, flat takeaway

1. **Taking the club back on an inside, flat plane**

The arms have lost their connection to the body.

2.   Letting the arms separate from the body

A weak position at the top with the club pointing well to the right

3.　**The club excessively across the line at the top**

The club laid off at the top of the backswing

4. **Having the club shaft point well left of the target at the top of the backswing (laid off)**

A long backswing with no width

5.   An overswing

On the downswing, the club is moving down on a plane that's too steep—a typical high-handicapper problem.

6. Starting the club down too steeply, leading to an out-to-in path

The club is too shallow from the inside coming into the ball—a typical low-handicapper problem.

7.   Halfway down, the swing plane is too shallow and the path is too much in-to-out.

The clubhead beating the hands into the ball—a weak scoopy action.

8. **Early release of the hands and club before impact—losing the lag**

Rolling the hands and forearms to square up the clubface

9. Trying to square up the clubface at impact with excessive club, hand, forearm, and wrist rotation

The radius of the swing is breaking down.

10. **A breakdown of the left arm through impact (chicken wing)**

Face open halfway down

Face closed halfway down

11. Difficulty squaring the clubface at impact because of the face position halfway down

Most of these faults I've mentioned tend to be an effect, not the cause, and trying to fix an effect is often a never-ending struggle. The good news is that the A Swing automatically eliminates many of these problems. It simplifies what the arms and club need to do to swing effectively and efficiently and allows the pivot to work better. It also makes it a lot easier to fix any problems when they do occur. That's a huge reason why the A Swing is so appealing when compared to the way most people try to swing the club. It's a problem-solver and a time-saver!

"OUT OF SYNC" BACKSWING

Early finish with the body pivot—arms and club incomplete

Arms and club at the top—body rotation incomplete

To consistently synchronize the pivot of the body with the swinging of the arms, I believe the club should travel the shortest distance possible to arrive at the top of the backswing, along the most direct route—this allows for the club to get to the top at about the same time as the body pivot completes, in other words both components reach their destination almost simultaneously. Problems with synchronicity occur if the body (shoulders and hips) finishes its motion in the backswing long before the arms and club arrive. Alternatively, the arms and club get to the top before the body has completed its journey. In both cases you have an "out of sync" swing. The A Swing greatly reduces the chance of either sync issue happening because the swinging of the arms and club is less complicated. When biomechanics expert J. J. Rivet tested the A Swing, he determined the butt end of a 6-iron traveled on average only thirty inches from address to the top of the backswing. That is six inches less than the butt end of the same club moved during a conventional backswing. The shortened distance of nearly 20 percent illustrates the A Swing's efficiency and makes it much easier to sync the arms with the

The rotation of the body and the swinging of the arms and club reach the top in sync—resulting in a short arm swing, but still a "full look."

pivot motion going back, therefore making it much easier to sync the two components coming down.

*Even though the arm swing is shorter in the A Swing, the club in most cases still has the appearance of being swung back fairly full, especially with the longer clubs. The cocking and loading of the wrists, combined with the pivot motion, creates this "full look."

The length of the journey of the club to the top of the backswing is crucial to your success, of syncing up your swing—the hallmark of the A Swing is that it eliminates wasted motion. Good players can generally handle it if their arms and club swing to the top on a route longer than necessary. They are able to compensate in many different ways to get back in sync during the downswing. Most golfers, however, who struggle to coordinate their pivot and arm swing during the backswing are, as a result, not able to get in sync on their downswing. In our testing, even good players who struggle with consistency have found that adopting the A Swing backswing makes overall syncing up so much easier.

The analogy I like for the efficiency of the A Swing backswing is that it's like flying from New York to Miami on a direct flight versus heading to Chicago first and then down to Miami. Either way you'll eventually get to Miami, but one route takes more time and you travel a lot farther to get there. In other words, it's a lot less efficient. So why fly to Chicago if you don't have to? The same holds true with the A Swing. No one can deny that if your arm swing is short and direct, then there is far less time for something to go wrong and the chance of your pivot and arm swing syncing are far greater.

For learning purposes, I'll break down the arms-and-club movement of the A Swing into the backswing and downswing sections, but they must ultimately blend into one flowing motion. A good downswing is largely the result of a good backswing—it's a chain reaction, and as the A Swing is largely based around the backswing, I will go into a lot of detail about how to perform it correctly. Your downswing will be a reaction to your backswing. It will utilize gravity and centrifugal force to hit the ball—it will be reactive and without much thought. The easiest way to explain what occurs and also help you learn the movements faster is to describe them in order. Follow this step-by-step approach.

THE BACKSWING

Move the club back with the belly/core.

- Starting from a solid foundation and utilizing the prayer grip, feel as if your belly/core (just like in the start to the pivot drill) moves away from the target while you push the club back slightly inside the target line for a short distance with your left hand and forearm. The left hand and wrist remain in a cupped position—the same as they were at address.

The clubhead stays outside the line of the hands on their respective lanes—clubface looks at the ball.

- Let your left arm move in and across the bottom of the chest. The clubhead has to stay outside the line of the hands (it does not move outside the target line), and this feel needs to be retained all the way to the top of the backswing. What do I mean when I say the clubhead should stay outside the line of the hands? Picture a running track. The hands move along the smaller inside lane and the clubhead runs along a larger outside lane. In other words, the hands are in, and the clubhead is out. The goal is to make sure that the hands and clubhead stay in their respective lanes as they swing to the top. This important concept is what gives the A Swing its distinct look of a steep shaft plane going back!

The right arm stays on top of the left with no forearm or club rotation.

■ **Ensure the right arm stays above the left arm all the way to the top of the backswing and and eliminate any rotation of the forearms or opening of the club.**

By the time the club reaches the top of the swing, the face hangs in a neutral or square position.

■ Without manipulating the clubhead, keep its face pointing at the ball for as long as you can during the early part of the backswing. Although the face will initially appear to be in a closed or shut position, it will end up in a neutral position by the time it reaches the top of the swing. This is as a result of the prayer grip and the steep plane of the shaft.

Loading the wrists about a third of the way back.

■ After you move the club about a third of the way back, start to load the wrists, particularly the right wrist (the prayer grip promotes this move). The palm of the right hand should be facing the ground as you hinge it. Remember to keep the clubhead outside the hands! To make sure you are loading the wrists, see that you have retained the prayer look in the grip (the cup at the back of both wrists).

The shaft is almost matching the angle of the spine and the left arm is pinned across the chest, one-third of the way back.

If you look at the shaft about a third of the way into the backswing, it should be leaning away from you almost parallel to your spine angle. Sense the left arm is pinned deep across the chest. This shaft position is very different from that in a traditional backswing, where it tends to lay down in the opposite direction. This is the essence of the A Swing.

The angle of the shaft halfway back in a conventional backswing plane looks dramatically different to the A Swing.

This difference is the key to shortening the club's journey to the top and achieving the compact look. The beyond vertical shaft angle going back will encourage the club to fall and shallow onto the proper plane during the downswing, which is the most important plane in the swing and where most golfers struggle.

The A Swing top of the backswing—compact and wound. The left arm lies under the shoulder plane. The club points slightly right of the target.

You should feel a pinching sensation between the inner right biceps and the chest.

- Maintain the connection of the left arm with your chest all the way to the top. Check to see that at the top the left arm lies under the shoulder plane, the club points a touch to the right of the target (the natural direction for it to point, by the way), and that the prayer grip is maintained to ensure a neutral clubface. Make no attempt to artificially extend or straighten the left arm on the backswing. Keep it soft and relaxed and with the correct move down, the left arm will automatically extend on the downswing, so it's straight where it counts—at impact. You should also feel a pinching sensation between the chest and the inside of the right biceps muscles at the top of the backswing. This connection helps keep the arm swing short and compact and maximizes the coil.

This backswing certainly is a change from conventional thinking—which is the point. It's an easier, more efficient way to get the club to the top in order to make the all-important downswing easier to perform. You might think, wow, this is different, but its concept is merely an evolution and extension to my thoughts and teachings through the years. For instance, I have always believed the clubhead should stay outside the hands to start the backswing (whipping the clubhead inside is one of golf's biggest faults). I have also always believed in the backswing plane's being steeper than the downswing plane (with the A Swing it's significantly steeper). I've always taught a full turn and a short arm swing, i.e., a compact swing. And I've always been an advocate of syncing up the swing—the body controlling the arms. So I don't feel I have strayed too far from my roots. The lack of rotation with the club and the feeling of keeping the clubhead outside the line of the hands all the way to the top is different, but this is how you shorten and simplify the motion. This is the direct route to Miami! The A Swing backswing looks and feels a little different, especially when rehearsing it at a slow speed. However, if you are watching it at normal speed, the club just looks a little more upright in the early part of the backswing. But in the business area—the downswing up to impact, I can assure you it is purely conventional. Here are some feels to help you with this new backswing.

BACKSWING FEELS

- The start of the swing is crucial, and you must resist the urge to pick the club up, push it outside the target line, or rotate it open with just your hands. When you move your core away from the target and push with your left hand back, the butt of the club should stay low and the clubhead should be looking at the ball.

- To sense the proper hinging and cocking action of the wrists, feel one hand working against the other in a push-pull sensation as the club swings away (push with the left and pull with the right). The two opposing forces create the proper loading action of the wrists without having to force things.

- For the pivot to control the swinging of the club, grip tension must remain light and the arms relaxed. The tempo of the swing can then be controlled by the pace of the pivot. Although the club is traveling a shorter distance and as a result arrives at the top sooner than it does in a conventional swing, you need to feel you are winding your torso slowly to maximize the coil and sync the swing. So take your time winding back.

- To swing back so the clubhead remains outside the line of the hands (hands in/club out), the butt end of the club has to move sharply inward as the left arm travels in and across the chest. Feel as if you are pointing the butt end of the club behind the right hip pocket.

- To get a feeling for the shape of the steeper backswing, and to keep the clubhead from going inside, make swings with your back to a wall. Stand with your heels about six inches away from the wall. Feel the butt of the club going in, and swing up with the club, avoiding the wall. Note: This is for the backswing only.

Keep the hands linked together all the way to the top.

- One of my favorite feel drills is called the push-palm and will help you get the winding/coiling sensation going back. Place the right hand under the left so the palms face in opposite directions and the back of the hands are linked together. Mimic a backswing by initiating the move with the core and stretching the right side up. Maintain this crossed-hand position while keeping the right arm higher than the left as you complete the wind of the upper body. Hold this coiled, top-of-the-backswing position for a few seconds to obtain the feel—body wound, arms relaxed.

Keep the item wedged into your right armpit as you swing back. It will ensure you wind your upper body to complete the backswing and not lift the arms to do so.

- **Place my Boomerang Training Aid (see "The A Swing Training Aids" at the end of the book) or a putter cutter deep into the right armpit. Make a backswing while trying to keep the item from falling. Feel the right biceps pinch against the chest as you reach the top of the swing. You will really feel wound, and keeping the item wedged into your armpit will make it impossible for the arms to lift independently. *Do not attempt to keep the right elbow close to your side to hold the item in place.* Only the upper arm pinches against the chest.**

These feels often accelerate learning because many golfers find it easier to sense a correct position rather than to follow detailed verbal instructions. These feelings can even be used on the golf course.

BACKSWING NUGGETS

- Keep the butt end of the club in and the clubhead out, all the way back.

- Have the clubface looking at the ball in the early stages of the backswing.

- Swing the left arm deep across the chest.

- Sense the shaft plane beyond vertical.

- Keep the right arm on top of the left.

- Set and load the wrists by the time you are a third of the way back to the top.

- Feel the length of the arm swing short and the club pointing a touch to the right of the target at the top.

- Pinch the inner biceps muscle of the right arm against the chest.

- Maintain the cup in both wrists—the prayer look.

- Relax the left arm and keep it below shoulder height at the top of the swing.

CONCLUSION FOR THE A SWING BACKSWING

The most important thing to remember is that the positions in the backswing are designed to make the all-important downswing easier to repeat, where the movement of the body takes on the major role. While these positions might seem unorthodox at first, they're actually natural and easy to get into. Batters in baseball hold the bat fairly upright until the ball is released by the pitcher because it feels natural to start from there before they move into the power position. They certainly don't start off waiting for the pitch with the bat parallel to the ground. The bat goes from a steep, vertical plane to a shallow one through the unwinding of the body—that's what needs to happen when you swing the club.

Another hallmark of the A Swing backswing is that it's impossible to overdo, so you'll see improvements in your shot-making even if you don't have it down 100 percent. Just improving it marginally will make your swing more efficient, more in sync, and more consistent—in other words, you will play better as you are working on it.

FREQUENTLY ASKED QUESTIONS ABOUT THE A SWING BACKSWING

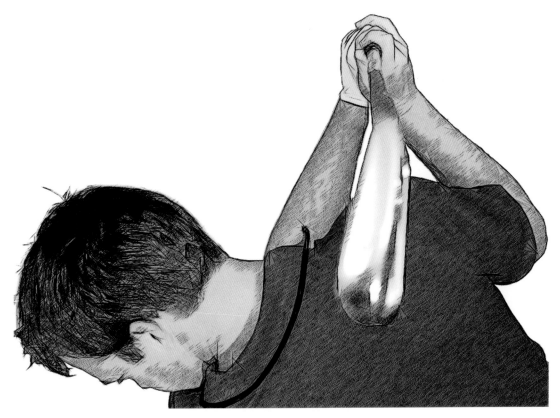

The vertical shaft plane results in a neutral position at the top.

Q. Isn't the clubface too closed going back?

A. It might seem that way initially, but because of the vertical nature of the shaft plane, it ends up in a neutral position at the top of the backswing. That is the only thing that matters. *The A Swing, which has essentially no shaft or face rotation on the backswing, is designed to set the shaft and clubhead in the proper position on the way down.*

The club goes from a steep plane going back to a shallow plane coming down.

Q. I thought the club-shaft angle halfway back needed to be on the same plane it was on at address. The A Swing has the shaft leaning in the opposite direction. Isn't that way too steep?

A. Conventional wisdom is to keep the club on the same plane during the backswing and the downswing as it started on at address. But that's easier said than done. In my opinion that approach, in most cases, makes the task of hitting good shots more difficult, especially for the average player. Many great ball-strikers of the past had varying degrees of a steep-to-shallow plane. Jack Nicklaus had the shaft pointing almost vertical halfway into the backswing. He would then shallow it naturally onto the correct plane coming down. Johnny Miller, one of the greatest iron players in history, had

a similar look to his swing. The Canadian golfer George Knudson, recognized as one of the finest swingers ever, also went from steep to shallow. Calvin Peete was known for his ultrasteep backswings and perfectly on-plane downswings and was one of the star players during the 1980s and 1990s. Ever since they started keeping statistical records on the PGA Tour, there has never been a more accurate hitter of the ball than Calvin Peete. He led driving accuracy and greens in regulation for almost ten years in a row. *Testing has shown that the A Swing backswing helps even the average golfer deliver the club onto the proper downswing plane. Being on plane coming down is the common denominator with all good players.*

A baseball hitter goes from steep to shallow as the pitch approaches.

The A Swing definitely has links to a batter's swing in baseball. Hitters wait for the pitch with the bat in an extremely vertical position. Their arms are soft and relaxed, and in most cases, the left arm is slightly bent. Then as the pitch approaches, they unwind their lower bodies, and dynamics and physics take over. The angle of the bat shallows onto the plane that the ball is moving on, and as a result of the forces created, the left arm straightens automatically—the bat lags behind the hands, which creates tremendous speed as contact is made with the ball—then the arms extend into the finish of the motion.

Illustrating the V plane

I have named this transition from steep midway during the backswing to on-plane midway into the downswing the V plane. If you looked at yourself in a mirror making this midswing change, the club shaft would approximately form the two sides of the letter V. On the backswing it would look like the left side of the letter, and on the downswing it would look like the right side.

It's not a perfectly symmetrical $\vee$, but it is a great image to understand how the shaft should move. This change of plane is important for the many golfers who lack energy and flow in their swing and swing steeply from out-to-in. The $\vee$ plane motion adds life and energy to the swinging action of the club and, also, based on J. J. Rivet's testing, aids in keeping the spine angle constant on the backswing and the downswing. This is an important factor in consistency, which is a problem for many golfers. Keep in mind that the transition part of the pivot motion plays the key role in this change of plane.

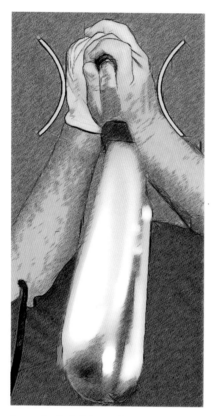

A neutral clubface linked with the "cupped" wrists at the top of the swing

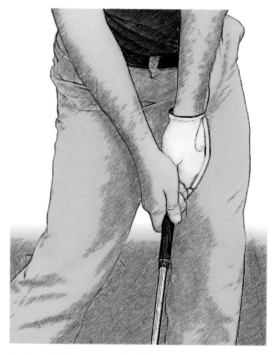

As the club approaches impact, the left wrist flattens or slightly bows for the briefest period before returning to a cupped position.

Q. **What is the purpose of maintaining a cupped left wrist at the top of the backswing? I thought it had to be flat.**

A. **To achieve a neutral clubface at the top of the backswing, you need to maintain the cup at the base of the left and right wrists—the prayer position you started with. This means there is no manipulation with the hands. Also, the cups are instrumental in the loading and cocking of the wrists to add power to the swing. Only through impact does the left wrist need to be in a flat or slightly bowed position.**

Q. I thought you were supposed to keep the left arm straight when you take the club back to create the widest swing arc possible. Why do you say the left arm should be soft and relaxed?

A. So much is said about the need for extension and width on the backswing, but this creates a lot of problems. Sure, the backswing has to have some width, and I am not suggesting you bend or collapse the left arm, but when golfers hear the word *extend*, they overuse their arms to achieve this extension to the detriment of setting the wrists and winding up the body, thus losing sync. True, many good players are really extended and wide as they swing to the top, but much of this is due to their great strength and flexibility. The majority of golfers, who struggle to have a synced-up backswing or do not possess those physical assets, will find the backswing easier to repeat and to sync up by having a feeling of a soft and relaxed left arm. They will then place more emphasis on winding the body and loading the club, which will, importantly, lead to good width and leverage on the downswing as the body and club unwind in sync at impact.

Q. Why does the A Swing have the club shaft pointing to the right of the target line at the top of the backswing? I thought the shaft needed to point on a line parallel to the target.

A. Many great players throughout history have had the club pointing right of the target at the top—known as being across the line. The list includes Bobby Jones, Jack Nicklaus, Tom Watson, and Tiger Woods in his early years. It's simply easier for most players to get on plane and swing from the inside coming down from this across-the-line position. It adds fluidity to the motion—especially if the distance the arms travel on the backswing is fairly short, as it is with the A Swing. When the left arm is snug to the chest and the shaft is steep, the rotation of the upper body naturally places the club slightly across the line. When the swing is ultralong and loose and across the line, problems occur. But if the swing is compact, it's beneficial to be in this position.

Q. The shaft swings back on a steep plane, but the arms swing back on a flat plane. Shouldn't they move on the same plane?

A. The steeper shaft position makes it easier to properly shallow the club on the downswing. And the flat arm swing connects them to the torso, so they can move in sync with the pivot motion. This A Swing would not be termed overly upright or flat when observing it—it's a combination of the two. I call it a flat-upright backswing. The arms are flat but the club is upright.

Q. What happens on the backswing if the left arm is not as inside or the shaft is not as steep as you suggest?

A. The beauty of the A Swing is that you will see improvement in your ball-striking as you work toward getting into the model backswing position. In reality, because of physical limitations or discomfort, you might never get into the exact model position—but that's okay, you don't have to be perfect! The key is to have the club as vertical as possible and the left arm as close as possible to your chest (short arm swing, full body rotation)—you can never overdo trying to exaggerate the feeling. That's what I like about it. It's all about being able to make a good transition into the downswing. Only a few people I have taught the A Swing do actually take the club back model-perfect, but the great thing about the A Swing is, the closer you get to the model, the more you will improve your synchronicity, consistency, and ball-striking regardless.

THE DOWNSWING

You have to consciously think about some things initially when learning the backswing, but the downswing, which takes about a third of the time to complete, is reactive. If your backswing is properly synced, your torso is wound, and the transition is good, the downswing will largely happen as a result of gravity and centrifugal force. Natural forces that impart flow and energy to the club will do the job. However, having an understanding of what takes place in what sequence is good, which is why I recommend rehearsing the downswing in slow motion to get the feel. The goal however, is to let the downswing happen simply as a reaction to the backswing—especially considering the short time it takes for the club to get back to the ball. Although I'm teaching you the backswing and downswing in segments, don't forget that you'll ultimately need to sync them into one continuous motion.

So what happens in that short time from the start of the downswing to the finish? Here is the sequence:

At the start of the downswing, the back of the left forearm and the palm of the right hand rotate slightly up toward the sky—which is part of the steep-to-shallow process in the A Swing.

■ Starting with the transition, the lower body moves toward the target just as the upper body and club are still completing the backswing. You'll recall from the pivot-motion chapter that I talked about increasing the differential between the hips and shoulders in the transition in order to generate power in the swing. This dynamic action gets the hands and club moving back down in tandem with a movement of the right shoulder and elbow. In conjunction with the body movement, the back of the left forearm and the palm of the right hand initially make a slight rotation up toward the sky, from the golfer's viewpoint. The shaft, which was steep and pointed across the line at the top, now flattens on to a shallower plane—so, no conscious rotation of the arms or club going back, but some rotation as you start down prior to their swinging to impact. This motion creates the other side of the letter \/. Try to picture this happening: from the top, the shaft moves from steep to shallow, and the left forearm makes a subtle rotation up toward the sky. This action provides some real life and flow into the club as it makes its downward journey.

Approaching halfway down, the shaft is flattening to the plane it started on.

■ As the club swings down, the shaft is now shallowing toward the plane that it laid on at address. This is one of the A Swing's most important benefits. Most amateurs never shallow the plane on the downswing. Their plane is far too steep. Good players shallow the club onto the plane it was on at the start, known as the original plane line. The shallowing or flattening of the shaft is also a prerequisite to syncing the arms and the body on the way down to impact.

The club is on plane, almost parallel to the right forearm as it swings down to impact.

■ Swinging down, the club is shallowing to get parallel to and above the original plane line—the correct angle to release the club from. The right elbow moves in front of and adjacent to the right hip, and as the club moves closer to impact, the shaft is almost parallel to the right forearm. This all happens as a result of the body's unwinding and the weight moving to the left side. The arms and club react to the body motion, and the club shaft now completely lies on the other side of the \/ plane.

The left forearm and palm of the right hand rotate down toward the ground to square the face off.

■ From here, to release the club and square the face off, the left forearm and the palm of the right hand now rotate down toward the ground, along with the straightening of the right arm. The body is beginning to clear out of the way as the arms and club accelerate through, with the hands leading the clubhead through to impact. The lagging clubhead approaches the ball on a path that is slightly from inside the target line.

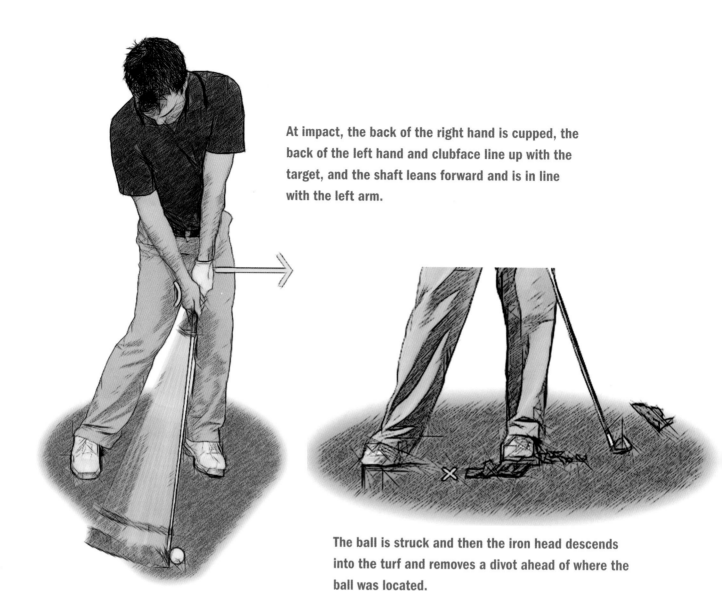

At impact, the back of the right hand is cupped, the back of the left hand and clubface line up with the target, and the shaft leans forward and is in line with the left arm.

The ball is struck and then the iron head descends into the turf and removes a divot ahead of where the ball was located.

■ By swinging down in the proper sequence, you will sync up the releasing club and the rotating body at the point of impact—where it counts. At impact, the chest is on top of the ball, the right arm has some flexion as the hands lead the clubhead, the right wrist is bent back or cupped, and the right palm pushes toward the ground. Conversely, the left wrist and back of the left hand are now flat or slightly bowed, as along with the clubface they line up toward the target (this hand position is essential for a piercing ball flight with the irons). With the shaft leaning toward the target and in line with the left arm, the clubhead makes contact with the ball and then descends into the turf, where a divot is then taken. The clubface is only on the target line for a brief moment in the impact area. Just past impact, the path of the swing then moves back inside the target line, mirroring its path into the ball.

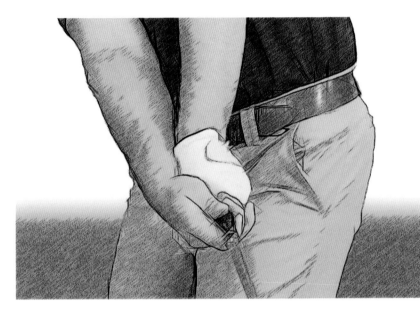

The post-impact position of the wrists is the opposite of the pre-impact position—right hand under, back of the left hand facing the sky.

■ After the ball has been struck, the post-impact position of the wrists is the opposite of the pre-impact position. Instead of the right wrist being bent back and the left wrist being flat or a little bowed, now the left wrist is bent back and the right wrist is bowed. This is the proper release pattern for the hands and ensures that the clubface remains square to the swing path as the right hand whips through.

The right-hand release has the same look as a left-hander approaching impact.

This release might feel different to what you are used to. Essentially, the right hand stays under the left instead of rolling over it, with the back of the left hand facing the sky. The position of the hands resembles the look of a left-handed golfer swinging into impact.

From just past impact into the follow-through, the arms and club are swinging around and to left of the body in unison with the rotation of the chest—if the chest stops, the hands and arms get too active.

The club rehinges into the finish as the wrists maintain their bent and bowed look.

The toe of the club points skyward halfway down and halfway through on matching planes.

- Both arms get fully extended for a brief period before the left arm begins to fold as the wrists maintain their bent-and-bowed appearance. The club has a rehinged look halfway into the finish (a mirror image of the hinging that took place during the backswing). From the golfer's viewpoint, the toe of the club will be pointing skyward just as it was halfway down. The downswing and follow-through planes of the club also have a matching look.

- As the swing finishes, the body stops rotating and the club, arms, and hands finish their journey—a sign of good synchronization. Typically the golfer should look as if he or she is posing for a picture, standing in balance, supported by the left leg, up on the toes of the right foot, and the club wrapped around the back of the neck, with the hands basically back in the original prayer position.

Finish the swing in balance, as if posing for a picture.

Unlike the backswing, which can be a bit mechanical, the downswing is free-flowing and dynamic. The energy generated by the body pivot moves into the arms and hands and is finally transferred into the club and the ball. This transfer happens most efficiently and effectively when the rotation of the body (the inner circle) moves in harmony with the swinging of the arms and club (the outer circle). Neither should outrace the other.

I am aware that was a lot to digest. Certainly I don't want you thinking about all of that—especially not in the short time it takes to make an actual downswing and follow-through. But it is important to know what happens sequentially. Remember, the downswing is largely reactive. It's the result of good sequencing and synchronization earlier in the swing. But having an understanding of it will help you learn the A Swing much faster.

Finally, just a word on an almost forgotten subject these days—hand action. Much of modern technique revolves around big muscle movement—we have discussed at length role a proper pivot motion plays in the A Swing. I also, though, place a lot of emphasis on correct hand action. We have referenced the hands and wrist action several times, and having an awareness of them is particularly vital coming into the ball, at, and just past impact. Ultimately, the hands control the clubface, affecting the shape and trajectory of the shot. The old adage that great players have great hands is true today as it ever was, and is an integral part of the A Swing.

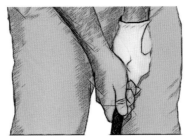

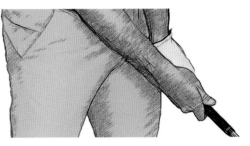

The right hand is back coming into the ball.

The left wrist is flat at impact.

The right hand is under the left after impact.

As I said at the start of this section, rehearse the downswing in slow-motion a number of times so you can recall what the correct positions fel like, and then incorporate them when you progress to full-speed swings. Remember that your goal is to make the downswing purely instinctive and automatic, and a reaction to all that has gone before!

DOWNSWING FEELS

The downswing is similar to the hand-and-arm action needed to skip a stone across water.

■ As the club approaches impact, sense you are trying to skip a stone across water. The shoulder is low and the right elbow is close to the hip and leads the hand.

The club travels on an arc from inside the target line before impact and after impact.

- Think of the clubhead as traveling along an imaginary arc such as the bottom of a Hula-Hoop or circle. During the downswing, the club moves toward the ball from inside the target line. At impact, the clubhead is on the target line, then during the follow-through, the club moves back inside the target line. If you visualize this Hula-Hoop lying at the same angle as your club, then make sure the clubhead moves along the curvature of the hoop before and after impact as it swings around to the left and then on to the finish.

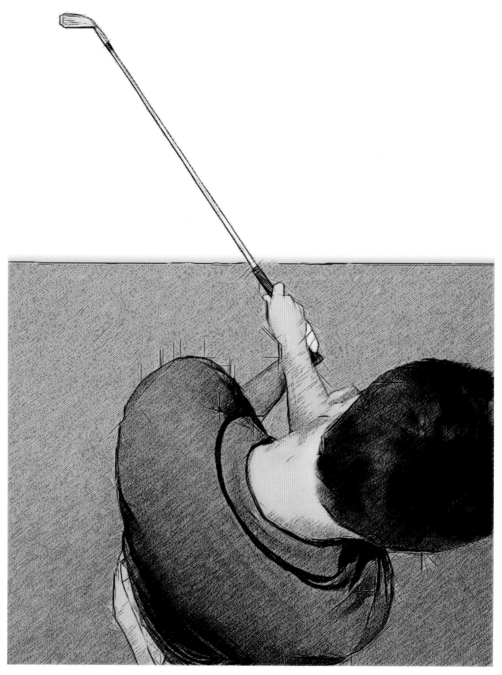

A very common release pattern that has been taught for years where the right hand
and forearm roll over the left and close the face

■ The right wrist is bowed under and the left wrist is cupped back after impact, with the
back of the left hand looking up at the sky. This position is quite different from how the
hands are typically taught to work in a traditional swing, where they roll over each other
and the back of the left hand faces the ground. In the A Swing, the right hand is under
the left, and its palm faces you halfway into the follow-through. The right-hand position is

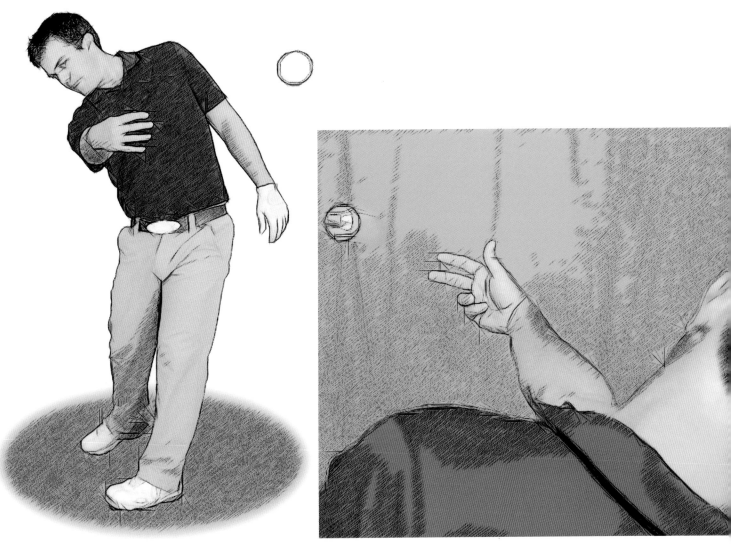

The release of the right hand is similar to releasing a ball.

similar to that of a shortstop in baseball after he throws the ball across his body to try to get a batter out at first.

- To allow the arms and body to work in unison, keep the chest moving all the way to the finish. If the chest stops, the hands and arms take over.

When looking halfway down, in a mirror, to be on plane, the club shaft should be parallel and above the Plane Tape.

- Place my easily removable Plane Tape (see "The A Swing Training Aids" at the end of the book) on a mirror to match your shaft at address—the original plane. While standing a few feet away from the mirror, make the A Swing backswing and then feel the club shallowing on the downswing back onto the original plane ($\bigvee$ plane).* Check that halfway into the downswing the club shaft looks parallel and slightly above the tape on the mirror. It should stay that way until it gets close to impact. That is the correct plane, and the club is in an ideal position to strike the ball. The club never wants to drop under the original plane line, as this means that the club has gotten *too* shallow—which good players tend to suffer from. The result is a path into the ball that is severely in-to-out.

* To have the perfect image of the $\bigvee$ plane, you can place a second piece of Plane Tape on the mirror to represent your A Swing backswing plane.

- Using a short iron, set up to a ball and make a backswing. Once you reach the top in a wound-up position, pause for a two count. Now let your lower body glide toward the target, unwind and strike the ball. Gliding before unwinding helps create the proper sequencing on the downswing—where the lower body leads the upper body, arms, hands, and club. Be patient hitting balls with this pause format. It's tough at first, but with a little practice starting off with a short iron, it will really give you the feel of a sequenced, synced-up downswing.

- Make a slow-motion swing and stop just behind the ball, feeling your impact position. Check that your weight is on the left leg, pressure is on the left heel, the hips are in an open, rotated position, the club shaft is leaning forward, and the left wrist is flat and the back of the left hand is facing the target. Hold this model position for a couple of seconds, then flick the ball forward using your belly, chest, and right arm. This drill requires some strength and coordination, and you won't be able to advance the ball far, but that's not the objective. The goal is to sense impact and feel that the rotation of the body and the release of the club are working in sync.

DOWNSWING NUGGETS

- Unwind with the lower body sensing the shaft flattening (the right side of the \/ plane).

- Feel the connection between the flexed right elbow and the hip.

- Think in-to-out path as the club approaches the ball.

- Let the hands lead the clubhead into impact (right wrist bent back).

- Extend the right arm and feel as if you're releasing the right hand through the impact zone, as if throwing a ball.

- Swing to the left of the target line after impact for any shot you are hitting down on and taking a divot.

- Keep the chest moving to the finish in sync with the arms, hands, and club.

- Hold a balanced finish position.

CONCLUSION FOR THE A SWING DOWNSWING

The old adage that a good backswing sets up a good downswing is true. It aids the correct sequence of motion for the club to return consistently to the ball. As the lower body unwinds, the arms, hands, and club follow in that order. Forces act on the club, and as long as rhythm and continual flow are good, the design of the club pretty much ensures that it does return consistently. When this is done correctly, power is created freely and with comparatively little effort. Although you have detailed knowledge of the positions on the downswing, the objective is to make a freewheeling swing with little thought of those positions. The swing, when in full flow, is like a train that passes through and doesn't stop at the stations en route.

FREQUENTLY ASKED QUESTIONS ABOUT THE A SWING DOWNSWING

Q. What happens to my downswing if I don't hit all the positions perfectly on the backswing?

A. The advantage of the A Swing is that you will see progress in your synchronization and ball-striking even if your positions aren't model perfect. Any slight improvement working on the A Swing backswing will give benefit. I have observed that students make great improvement in their ball-striking while they are working toward the model—it's also virtually impossible to overexaggerate the feelings in working on the A Swing. For example, in the early stages of working on the backswing, it could well be that you will only achieve a mild version of the A Swing—the shaft might not be as angled or vertical as in the model. But trust me, as you keep working on it, it will tend to take on more of the model look, and your swing will become more efficient as the club travels on that shorter route—making the correct downswing, specifically the \\/ plane, easier to achieve. The key on the backswing is to have the club as vertical as you can with the left arm deep (short arm swing, but full body rotation) with the club slightly across the line. But even if you aren't picture-perfect, you'll still be in a good position to make an improved, shallower downswing. Think about the \\/ plane we have spoken about— steep to shallow.

 MODEL A SWING   MILD A SWING

Even if you are not in the perfect A Swing position on the backswing and you have the "mild" version, you will still see great improvement in your synchronization and ball striking.

You could also end up with only a "mild" version of the A Swing, as this is all you need to get in better sync. I have students that get into the full version completely, and others, even when they are feeling exaggerated in a practice swing, end up in a mild version when they hit the ball. This is the beauty of the A Swing. Doing it completely or partially brings great benefits, and through practice and trial and error, you will see benefits, too. The goal is to follow the recipe, and wherever the backswing ends up eventually, it is your personalized version of the A Swing! Remember, we are all different, and there are never going to be two exact swings, even though the thoughts behind them may be the same. One of the benefits with the A Swing is that I have not seen any student overdo any facet of it. As a consequence, the feelings never get old—you can keep working on them and trying to exaggerate them. With most swing feels, they tend to last a while, then you need new ones—not the case with the A Swing. How comforting is it to know you can keep the same keys and never overdo them!

Q. I've always been told that it's bad for the left wrist to cup or break down coming into impact. Is that not flipping or scooping? Shouldn't my hands and arms roll over one another to square the face off?

A. You are correct if you are talking about having the left wrist cupped before impact. I am talking about the wrist's being cupped after impact. I certainly don't want you to try to help lift the ball in the air by making a scooping motion with your wrists and hands prior to contact. Your goal is to hit down on the ball and then take a divot. To achieve this, at the precise point of impact and just past it, the left wrist is flat or bowed slightly forward, and the right wrist is cupped back. Just beyond impact, however, when the ball has left the clubface and both arms have extended, the release of the right hand, in conjunction with the straightening of the right arm, causes the left wrist to cup so that the back of the left hand faces the sky. This enables one to keep the clubface square to the swing arc, which is crucial for accuracy and also speed, as the right hand whips through. Keep in mind how a left-handed golfer would look with his wrists as his club is approaching the ball. The right wrist is flat or bowed and the left wrist is cupped back. It's basically a mirror image of the right-handed golfer's post-impact release position using the A Swing.

This release pattern in the A Swing will feel different at first, as traditional instruction has for years taught that the forearms roll over each other and the back of the left hand should face the ground. You see this with a lot of golfers who, for various reasons, hit the ball to the right, so they desperately try to close the face with the rolling action. You also see it with good players who "hold off" their release coming into the ball (which takes strength) because they are wary of going left. Then well after they have struck the ball, forces applied to the clubhead create a rolling effect with the wrists and forearms, but fortunately, in most cases, the ball has long gone. With the release I'm suggesting, there is no "hold off" or conscious rolling of the forearms—just a full-flowing release with the right hand, as in throwing a ball. There are certainly situations, though, where there may be a case to encourage a rolling of the left forearm and wrist and a closing-down of the clubface in order to hit either a controlled low shot or to accentuate a draw, but these are speciality shots.

THE A SWING SUMMARY

This chapter is the heart and soul of the A Swing. I recommend you read it and study the pictures often, so that you are clear on the concept of what the club is doing in relation to the body and the track that it travels on. **The key is getting a feel for the backswing.** Do it well, and the downswing, along with the pivot motion, will seem to come naturally. Although the A Swing might feel different initially—most swing changes do—it won't take long before you realize how easy it is to do, and, more important, to repeat.

I'm not naïve enough to think that the A Swing will be universally accepted or suit everybody. Remember, it's an *alternative* approach. If you've struggled to improve using a traditional swing, then this might be your answer. If you're wondering if any of my most famous students have tried it—from Sir Nick Faldo to Nick Price to Michelle Wie—I can say yes, they have all used portions of it in their games with great success. My work with those players was, and still is, based on having a solid setup, emphasizing body rotation, a compact swing, steepening then shallowing the swing plane, and most of all having good synchronization—all hallmarks of the A Swing. That's why I have no doubt that the majority of golfers will see benefit from adopting the A Swing. Your swing will become more efficient and be more in sync. If you work on the feels to develop the motion, then apply the seven-minute plan in chapter 7, you'll be well on your way to mastering the A Swing and playing the consistent golf that you have always been seeking.

As I mentioned in the introduction, the A Swing is a great alternative for a wide range of golfers. The swing is so user-friendly that once you try it and get a feel for it, your confidence and consistency will soar, which will lead to lower scores and more fun. And if things do go a little awry, as they tend to do from time to time in this game, your knowledge of the A Swing will help you root out the problem and fix it in a flash.

This chapter will help you put the A Swing into action and also enhance your knowledge of it so you can really see some benefits. I've also included a troubleshooting guide to overcome many common problems. Now you have everything you need to play your best golf.

CHAPTER 6

UTILIZING THE A SWING

GETTING THE SWING STARTED

One of the difficulties in developing a fluid, consistent swing is that you're trying to hit a stationary ball. In other ball-and-stick sports, you're trying to hit a moving object, and the body intuitively reacts to perform the required motion. The action in these sports usually happens too fast for the conscious mind to get involved. Instincts tend to rule the day. That's not the case in golf. Starting the swing from a standstill, you have to perform a fairly complex series of movements in about a second. You have so much time prior to the swing to overthink the situation and let the conscious mind interfere with your body's natural athletic ability.

So how can you overcome this hurdle and make your swing fluid and reactive from the start? I recommend using a simple routine in preparation to getting the club started back smoothly and in sequence—it's all part of what is termed **a preshot routine.** It is a way to add motion and eliminate the tension that builds if you simply stared down at the ball and freeze at address, as many golfers do. Tension is a real killer in the golf swing.

Good players' routines vary but the key is they do them consistently on each swing. The best routines are generally brief, because the longer it takes to get the swing started, the greater the chance for cumbersome swing thoughts to manifest. These ruin its fluidity. I'm sure that you've heard the expression **paralysis by analysis.** That refers to overthinking, particularly at address. Any golfer who stands over the ball for several seconds before swinging, you can bet there's a lot of brain activity. It's so hard to get any rhythm or flow when that happens.

If you already have a preshot routine that you're comfortable with, and you do it consistently, then stick with it. But if, like most golfers, you don't have one, here is a plan that works well with the A Swing. Once you have looked at your target from behind the ball and visualized the shot, follow these steps:

1. **Walk up to the ball and get into your setup position.**

2. **Focus your eyes slowly on the target, then back to the ball. You can shuffle your feet a little to help alleviate tension.**

3. **Keeping your arms relaxed, rehearse the start of the A swing. Use your core muscles/belly to get the hands and the club moving a short distance, to where the grip of the club travels to or a little past your right thigh. Your left arm should feel linked to your chest, and your hands should be in close to your body—this movement is a form of waggle, but with no opening of the club or rolling of the forearms.**

4. **Return to the starting position. Slowly look back to the target and then return your eyes to the ball.**

5.   **After a slight hesitation, start the swing in the manner you just rehearsed.**

You can practice this system by initially counting off each step in your head. It won't take long to develop, and the process should soon become automatic. When this happens, you can go on the course and have no conscious thought of how or when you start the club back. You'll simply react and go. This gives you the best chance of having a free-flowing swing.

FINDING YOUR RHYTHM

I think of good rhythming as being how all of the pieces of the swing fit together into a fluid motion. There should be no rush or appreciable effort in the swing until around impact, when the clubhead whips and whooshes through the hitting area. For most golfers, their rhythm comes and goes. The swing can be relaxed and flow one moment, then tight and jerky the next. You'll even hear pros say that they didn't hit the ball well because their rhythm was off. Rhythm is certainly a big key to consistency. Here are two things you can do to aid your rhythm:

1. **Reduce tension by focusing on your breathing.** *Do not hold your breath at address.* **Instead, take a deep breath in through your nose, and then, just prior to swinging the club, open your mouth and start exhaling. Let it continue smoothly throughout the swing. Time it so that when you've finished the swing, you've completely exhaled. If your breathing is smooth, your swing will be smooth.**

Start the flow drill with the club ahead of the ball. Move the club away using your core muscles and then complete the whole swing and strike the ball.

2. **Put flow into the whole swing.** This drill is an old favorite of mine. Using a 7-iron or 8-iron, position the club as the shaft is pointing outside your left thigh and the clubhead is hovering off the ground a few feet ahead of the ball. Instead of starting your swing from the normal address position, initiate your backswing from here using your core muscles while keeping the arms relaxed. Starting the swing in front of the normal address position gives it momentum and flow. As you near the completion of your backswing, get your lower body moving forward while your upper body, arms, and club are still going back. This subtle change of direction adds so much energy to the swing and, if done in a fluid manner, creates tremendous clubhead speed. It's like a good casting motion in fly-fishing. As the right arm and shoulder come forward to cast, the fishing line is still moving backward. But then as it changes direction, it whips forward with great speed. This change of direction shouldn't feel violent or forced. If you stay relaxed, this drill is an excellent way to develop good rhythm and flow from start to finish. It's the way to achieve one of my favorite sayings in golf: *Swing easy and hit hard!*

TEE SHOTS

Sweep the ball off the tee with a slightly ascending angle.

When you're hitting an iron, hybrid, or a fairway wood off the turf, you have to strike the ball with a slightly descending blow. **But when the ball is sitting up on a tee and you're using a driver or a fairway wood, the goal is to hit it with a slightly ascending blow.** The A Swing, with its **V** plane, encourages this sweeping, upward angle of attack, which increases distance (carry and roll) by raising the launch angle of the shot and reducing spin. Here are the keys you need to hit long, solid tee shots.

1. **Widen your stance beyond shoulder width. It should be about three or four inches wider than if you were using a 6-iron. This will improve your stability while swinging the longer club.**

Lean the shaft so your hands are a little behind the ball's position.

2. Address the ball farther forward in your stance so it's approximately in line or close to your left heel or opposite your left armpit. Make sure it's teed high enough so the top half of the ball is above the top of the clubface.

3. Set your left hip even higher and your right hip lower than your normal 6-iron address posture. Make sure your spine is tilted away from the target, and that your sternum is behind the ball. With your left hip set high and the ball forward, you will have a touch more of your body weight (about 55 to 60 percent) supported on the right foot.

4. Lean the shaft of the club slightly away from the target at address so your hands are level with or a little behind the ball's position—with an iron, the hands are slightly ahead.

Note the difference in the body positions just past impact with an iron versus a driver—spine more vertical with the iron, and angled away from the target with the driver.

Now that you've altered your setup to promote an upward strike, it's time to maximize your power by tweaking the pivot motion. When hitting the driver, the pivot motion changes somewhat from what you have learned in chapter 4 in relation to the downswing, to accommodate your hitting up on it. **As you are swinging down and your hands are approaching about hip height, thrust your body upward just before impact.** Your head, as a result, will move farther back to the right. You'll end up being a little taller at impact than you were at address (in the iron swing you retain your address position at impact); and your spine will be angled away from the target. This impact position gives you room to get your arms extended past impact, imparting maximum speed. Compared to when you are hitting down on the ball with an iron, where you maintain your height and spine angle at impact, the shaft of the driver

should not be leaning toward the target as much. The shaft should, in fact, be nearly perpendicular to the ground to accommodate the sweeping, upward blow. You should also sense, as the cliché goes, that you are staying behind the ball with the driver, compared to being more on top of it with an iron.

With our biomechanical testing with top players, staying more behind the ball with the driver compared to the iron is clearly seen. Approximately 60 percent of the body weight is on the left side with the driver, whereas it is 80 percent with the iron.

This upward thrust of the body is powerful and is similar to the motion you would make if you squatted down and then jumped off the ground using your legs and core muscles. This can certainly be seen in Tiger Woods's swing, as well as in the swings of many long-drive

Practice this upward thrust using the pivot drill.

champions. Big hitters use the ground for leverage to generate maximum clubhead velocity. By thrusting upward, you'll not only gather a lot of energy that you can transfer into the hit, but you'll also assist the club to ascend through impact. This thrust move is similar to what lumberjacks do when they chop down a tree. Their bodies straighten as the ax hits the wood. That's the feeling you want.

To practice this move, rehearse the pivot-motion drill without a club. Take your setup with your arms folded and make a coiled backswing. As you unwind and are pivoting into the simulated impact zone, feel you're getting taller and straightening your spine. This is where you'll thrust up.

Keep in mind that this move happens in a flash as you shift your weight and rotate your body toward the target. The sensation is that your right hip and buttock are pushing forward out toward the target line as you move off your right foot. This movement is all about timing. You stay low initially as you start your downswing, then you spring up. You'll be amazed at how fast the club moves through the hitting area. As opposed to swinging an iron on a downward angle, where you feel the club moving left through impact, the sensation you'll have with a driver is that you're swinging a little more in-to-out, or right of the target. This helps promote a draw and even greater distance.

I have always believed that golf has basically two swings—one for the descending swing as with the irons, and one for the ascending swing as with the driver. Both backswings are the same, but the downswings are different. Understanding the differences will allow you to be more consistent with your whole game.

FAIRWAY WOODS AND HYBRIDS OFF THE TURF

Your goal is to hit slightly down on the ball with these clubs, just not as much as with an iron. This is especially true off a fairly tight lie. When using a fairway wood or hybrid, adjust your driver stance by narrowing it a couple of inches, playing the ball back a bit and setting your weight even on both feet. The pivot motion and the swinging of the club are just as prescribed in the previous chapters. The key with these shots is to keep the spine angle constant and stay down with the shot through impact. There's no upthrust motion as there is with the driver, which would result in topping shots. You should at least graze the grass with the clubhead as you squeeze the ball off the turf with a slight descending blow. The common mistake is to try to help the ball into the air, which leads to fat and thin shots. You have to trust that the design of these clubs will get the ball airborne.

PITCH SHOTS

The pitch swing in many ways is just a mini-version of the full swing. It also requires a solid foundation, a good pivot, and a steep-to-shallow swing plane—although the angle of the backswing plane is not quite as exaggerated as it is in the full swing and the club does not shallow as much. The pitch swing is shorter, more controlled, less dynamic, and based on rhythm. These are shots in the thirty- to one-hundred-yard range, the distance where the pros excel in terms of scoring. Here are the keys to hitting a pitch:

1. **Narrow your stance. The closer you get to the green, the narrower your stance gets, to the point where your feet are only a few inches apart when hitting the shortest of pitches and chips.**

2. **Address the ball in the middle of your stance with roughly 60 percent of your body weight on your left side. This will help you hit down on the ball for better contact.**

3. **Grip down on the club about an inch for better control.**

Although the lower body is aligned left (open) when pitching, the right foot is pulled back in a closed position—clubface aiming to the right.

4. Just like at address in the full swing, pull your right foot back, but rotate both feet and the rest of your lower body slightly to the left of the target. Your shoulders should stay fairly square. Having the right foot pulled back helps prevent you from spinning out with your knees and hips and cutting weakly across the ball with the club.

Open the face of the club and then take your grip.

5. **Open the face of the wedge a few degrees before you take your grip so it's pointing just right of your target at address.**

You need to open the face a touch (approximately ten degrees) because the length of a pitch swing is abbreviated. Let me explain. When you're hitting full shots using the A Swing, remember that the clubface appears closed in the early stages of the backswing, but ends up in a neutral or square position when it reaches the top. But with a compact pitch swing, say swinging it halfway back, the slightly open clubface at address ensures that the face remains neutral at the top of the shorter swing. If the face was indeed closed halfway back, you would then have to manipulate the clubface back to square on the way down to impact—not easy to do in such a short motion.

The pitch backswing—less exaggerated plane—neutral face

The pitch-swing backswing I would consider a "mild" version of the A Swing model. The same feelings still apply regarding the pivot motion; the hands-in, clubhead-out on the backswing; and the shaft's shallowing on the downswing. However, on the backswing, if the plane of the shaft at the completion point, say one-half or three-quarter length, is pretty much straight up and down (as opposed to leaning, as in the full swing) and then it shallows subtly onto the proper plane as it changes direction, you will have a consistent pitching action. You could say this is a narrower version of the \/ plane! In this mild version of the backswing, as a result of the shorter, smoother, less dynamic swing, you don't have the time and do not have the need for the planes to change that aggressively to get the club into a good position at impact and develop a repeating pitching motion.

With pitching, work on half and three-quarter swings, matching the follow-through length with the backswing.

As with the full swing, the pitch is controlled by the pivot motion, which, along with varying the clubs, establishes your different distances. All you have to do to vary the length of the shot is to experiment with the amount of the rotation of the pivot. The degree of pivot controls how far the arms swing back and how far you hit the shot. Practice pitch shots with a lob, sand, gap, or pitching wedge, pivoting so the left arm swings back until it is parallel to the ground (a half swing) or a little farther back for longer shots (a three-quarter swing). These are the two lengths of backswing I recommend you practice and stick with. Remember to match the backswing length to the follow-through length, and keep the swing smooth at all times. A good swing thought is to keep your chest continually rotating back and through. You never want to be too aggressive with these clubs. It's all about control. To hit a longer pitch it's far easier to swing smoother and just take an extra club than it is to swing harder with the same club. Try to take a nice, shallow divot, which imparts the right amount of spin to the shot. Take note of how far the ball goes when you vary the length of the swing with each wedge, and remember those distances when you play. Good wedge play is all about distance control.

Working on your pitching will improve your scoring, but it's also a great way to improve your synchronicity and technique for the full shots. Hitting solid pitches breeds confidence for when you get longer clubs in your hands and make the full A Swing—so get practicing these shots.

SHAPING SHOTS

Once you become a skilled player, one of the challenges of the game is to be able to execute shots that fit the situation. The A Swing is designed to hit the ball solidly and fairly straight (maybe favoring a slight draw, a right-to-left shape, but not a lot of curve). However, at times a good player will intentionally want to put more curve on the ball to the left or right. You might have to draw or fade a tee shot with a driver on a dogleg hole to maximize distance, or to access a tucked pin on the left or right edge of a green. Wind can also force you to curve the ball to help neutralize its effect—for example, draw the ball into a left-to-right breeze. One of the most satisfying aspects of the game is to pull off a shot that the circumstances or conditions require. Many golfers do not have the ability to intentionally shape shots, but it's a goal to work toward. Once you are seeing consistency in your shot patterns with the A Swing, the next big step up the ladder is to learn to control the shape of shots, and that's a lot of fun.

The following description might sound a little complex, but it's important to know the physics that make the ball curve. The curvature of the shot is mainly determined by the relationship of two things—the club path of the club and the position of the clubface at impact. The clubface essentially controls the initial direction of the shot, and the club path affects the curvature on the shot—both factors making the ball move right to left in the air (ideally starting to the right of the target and coming back to it); or left to right (the ball starting to the left of the target and moving back toward it). This has all been proven by modern launch monitors and debunks a lot of the old theories of how shots are shaped.

The good news is that you don't have to make major changes to your swing to shape shots. You can produce either a draw or a fade simply by making adjustments at address. To draw the ball (right to left), the club has to be swinging on a more in-to-out path in relation to the target line. In other words, the club has to be moving to the right of the target through the impact zone for a right-handed golfer to draw a shot. In addition to this path, the clubface needs to be slightly open (pointing right) in relation to the target line. But here's the important part. The face has to be closed, or aimed left, in relation to the club path. **So remember: face open to the target line, but closed in relation to the club path.** It's key to realize the difference between the target line—a straight line from the ball to the ultimate target; and the the swing-path line—the track that the clubhead travels on as it gets close to impact. If the clubface was closed to the target line at the point of impact, the ball would start to the left of the target as opposed to the right. The amount of draw is determined by how much in-to-out the club is swinging and also the degree the clubface is open. To hit a draw that returns to the target line, the face angle just needs to be pointing a little less to the right of the target at impact than

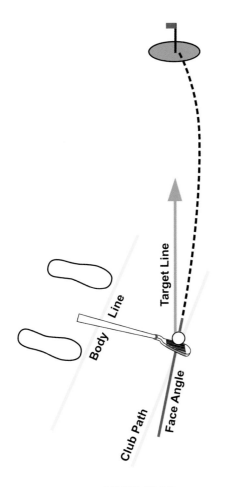

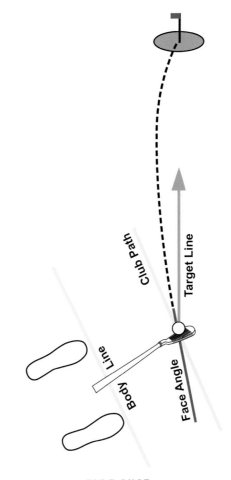

DRAW SHOT

Align your body and clubface to the right of the target for a draw in a 2:1 ratio—example, 10° right with your body - 5° right with the face.

FADE SHOT

Align your body and clubface to the left of the target for a fade in a 2:1 ratio—example, 10° left with your body - 5° left with the face.

the direction the club is swinging on. For example, if the club is swinging on an in-to-out path at an angle of ten degrees, then the face angle should be approximately pointing five degrees to the right at impact—a good rule of thumb is a 2:1 ratio. A nice image to hit the draw shot is that with an in-to-out path, the clubface from its open position is "closing" through impact, as opposed to being "closed"!

Conversely, for a fade—the ball starting left of the target and curving back to it—the opposite is true. With the club swinging out-to-in, the clubface has to be closed or pointing a bit left of the target line at impact. But remember, it has to be open, or aimed right, relative to the club path—**closed to the target line, open to the club line!** If the clubface was open to the target line at impact, the ball would start way right of the target and slice away from it. The amount of fade depends on the degree of the out-to-in club path. Once again, the 2:1 ratio applies. If the club is swinging on a path ten degrees out-to-in, and the face angle is five degrees left of the target line, then a fade should appear. The image of the clubface "opening" coming into impact, as opposed to being "open," is a good one to visualize.

I hope this explanation of curvature is clear, and you might have to reread this section a couple of times, but suffice it to know that you don't have to consciously change your swing to shape shots. As I said, it's all done through your alignment at address. So now, let's forget the theory and physics lesson and simply follow this recipe:

When addressing the ball, just make a couple of adjustments from your regular, square setup to hit an intentional draw or fade. Focus on aiming the body—the shoulders, hips, and knees—and for consistency, as with your regular setup, keep the right foot pulled back a bit for either shot. Remember, the feet don't affect the outcome of the shot. To draw it, aim your body and clubface right of the target, still using the 2:1 ratio. As an example, if your body is pointing ten degrees to the right of the target, set the clubface so it's only pointing five degrees right, closed in relation to the stance. With a fade, the opposite applies—aim your body ten degrees left of the target and the clubface five degrees left, open in relation to the stance.

With these adjustments in place, make your normal swing. Your body and clubface alignment will cause the ball to curve. Some tour players move the ball back a touch in their stance for a draw, and forward for a fade, which you can experiment with. But apart from this, you don't have to do anything else—though it never hurts to visualize the shape of the shot! When practicing, put two alignment sticks down on the ground—one to represent the target line, and the other for your adjusted body alignment. It's also easy to see with these sticks on the ground where your clubface is pointing. When possible, it helps to have somebody stand behind you to check the aim of your clubface and body when working on shaping shots—but tell the person not to worry about your feet!

I encourage you to experiment on the range to see how much of a draw or a fade your swing produces when aiming a certain amount right or left. Remember a couple of final points with this aspect of the game. Because of the amount of backspin that short irons impart (8-iron through wedges), it is hard to curve them, so 7-iron and down is the rule. Shaping shots with control is also based on hitting the ball out of the middle of the clubface—toe shots or heel shots can accentuate right-to-left and left-to-right spin, respectively. This part of the game should only be looked at once you are consistent with your ball-striking.

Okay, last bit of advice—only attempt these shots on the course after you have practiced them! Once you get to this point in your journey, you will know that your game is on the up-and-up!

TROUBLESHOOTING THE A SWING

The A Swing approach comes with a toolbox that allows you not only to build your repeatable golf swing, but to repair it when things break down. As good as it is, at times this will happen, believe me. Although you have an easy blueprint to follow, the A Swing is still an intricate movement that will occasionally need a tune-up. Being able to identify and correct your faults is an important part of owning the A Swing. When things do go wrong, the A Swing's simplicity makes it easy to get back on track quickly. I suggest you video your swing from time to time and see how it matches up to the model in the book, and also just as important, to see if what you are doing and what you feel you are doing are the same!

Here are ten of the most common problems I have seen golfers encounter when learning and using the A Swing, and what to do to fix them. These are mainly remnants of their old swings. Remember, in golf, old habits die hard.

1. **FAULT: The hands and arms push and lift the clubhead outside the target line at the start of the backswing.**

   FIX: After setting up in good posture, the core muscles of the stomach (belly) have to initiate the backswing. This results in the clubhead's moving away low and inside the target line, yet outside the line of the hands. This is a key factor in swinging the club back smoothly on a direct route to the top and in sync with the rotating body.

   CHECK: That you are initiating the backswing with the core to get the clubhead moving away low and inside the target line.

2. **FAULT: Rolling the forearm and club back inside the target line at the start.**

   FIX: Excessively rotating the forearm and club open going back leads to many issues in the swing and makes it difficult to square the clubface at impact. The goal is to have no rotation going back. Keep the left arm linked to the chest and have the clubface pointing at the ball as the club moves back. Keep the right arm above the left the entire time as the clubhead stays outside the line of the hands. You can check if you have too much rotation by viewing your swing in a mirror opposite you. Halfway into the backswing, you don't want to see that your right elbow is below the left. It must be above it.

   CHECK: That the left arm is linked to the chest, the clubface is looking at the ball, and the right arm is on top of the left.

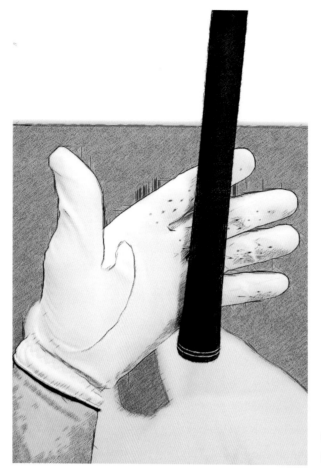

Check that the club lies down
toward the fingers of the left hand.

3. FAULT: Improper wrist action during the backswing (limited set) and the downswing
    (early uncocking).

    FIX: Get leverage in your swing by cocking and loading the wrists during the back-
    swing, then retaining that wrist cock for as long as possible during the downswing. It's
    essential to create leverage and to hit the ball solidly that you check your left-hand grip
    frequently. Make sure the handle lies diagonally down in the fingers and not too high in
    the palm (gripping it in the palm inhibits wrist action). Also make sure the right hand
    sits on top of the left—the prayer grip. This will encourage the left wrist to cock as
    the right wrist hinges back. *Loading the wrists going back helps delay their uncocking
    during the downswing until as late as possible creating lag in the swing, which leads to
    greater clubhead speed.*

    CHECK: That the club lies diagonally and partially across the fingers and palm of the
    left hand and that the right hand sits on top. The right wrist loads going back and that
    loaded position is held for as long as possible coming down.

Wind the upper body over a stable lower body.

4.   FAULT: **No coiling in the backswing.**

FIX: **To create power, you have to wind your torso going back. The goal is to stretch those big back muscles against the resistance of a solid lower body. When rehearsing the first part of the pivot motion, coil is achieved by the core's turning back with the left shoulder tilting down and the right shoulder and hip rising up. The upper body completes its rotation while the lower body stays quiet and stable. The more flexible you are, the easier it is for this to happen. If you aren't that flexible, to aid the rotation the left heel can lift, and that's okay as long as the left knee doesn't get overactive. Go back to rehearsing the pivot motion without a club until you can duplicate this coiled feeling when you swing.**

CHECK: **That at the top of the backswing, the left shoulder is turned down and the upper body feels wound against a stable lower body.**

5. **FAULT:** Synchronization issues. The pivot motion finishes before the arms and club get to the top. Or the arms and club swing all the way back to the top before the pivot completes.

    FIX: To improve the synchronization of your backswing, which leads to greater consistency, let the pivot motion of the body guide the arms and club to the top. The wrists need to be cocked and loaded early, the shaft needs to be steep and angled away from you on the \\/ plane, and your left arm connected to your upper body. Now as you reach the top of the swing, make sure you feel a pinching sensation between the biceps of your right arm and the chest. This will make your swing feel compact (a short arm swing). Focus on the pivot action's and the swinging of the club's finishing their journey to the top at the same time (the main feature of the A Swing is to fix this fault—a major reason for bad golf.)

    CHECK: That your wrists are fully cocked a third of the way into the backswing. The club shaft must be in a steep position (\\/ plane). The body rotation and swing of the club complete in unison at the top.

6. **FAULT:** A long and loose backswing.

    FIX: It's common for younger players or overly supple golfers to swing the club back too far. This longer swing can create synchronization issues and inconsistency. One of the great features of the A Swing is its compactness—getting the golfer fully wound up with the arm swing being of short length. If you have followed the backswing guidelines and yet your swing is still long and a little loose, that means you are late starting the downswing. The lower body needs to start forward toward the target earlier or sooner. Allow the lower body to glide smoothly toward the target as you are finishing the backswing. This dynamic move will put the brakes on the arms and shorten the swing. Think about it—how far can you keep going back if you are going forward?

    CHECK: That you time your lower body to go forward just before you complete the backswing with your hands and arms.

Start the anti-slice step drill from a narrow stance.

As you reach the top of the swing, sidestep toward the target with your left foot returning the feet to the standard width. This will teach you to shallow the plane.

7. **FAULT:** Hitting slices and pulls (the ball starts left of the target). These two faults are commonly referred to as being *over the top* or *swinging outside in.*

FIX: Although the ball flights are different, slices (the ball curves way right of the target) and pulls (the ball flies straight left of the target) are produced by the same mistakes. The downswing plane is too steep and the club moves on an out-to-in path across the target line. Whether a slice or a pull is produced depends on where the clubface is pointing when the ball is struck. For right-handed golfers, if the clubface matches the out-to-in path, you'll hit a pull. But if the face is pointing right or open in relation to this leftward path, you'll hit a slice. To fix either issue, focus on the \/ plane. Remember that the swing plane is steep going back and shallow coming down, and not the reverse, which is typical of slicers. This shallow downswing plane allows the club to move on the proper path from inside the target line. *As you reach the top of your swing, you want to shift your weight toward the target*—just as it does in the pivot drill. This will shallow the downswing and put the club on the proper plane and path. Your lower body has to lead the way. If you're still struggling to feel the shallowing of the shaft plane, here's a great drill: Set up to the ball with a narrower stance than normal. You still want your right foot dropped back in relation to the left, but slide your left foot in so it's closer to the right. Now make a swing, and just as you are completing the backswing, sidestep smoothly toward the target by returning the left foot to its proper position. If it's done correctly, you will feel that all important move, that you are shifting toward the target with the lower body as you are still going back with the upper body. This powerful move will shallow the downswing plane automatically and get the club coming from the inside, which eliminates slices and pulls. This drill also helps fault #6. (Do it initially without a ball.)

CHECK: That the club shaft is steep going back, but shallows when you start the downswing with your lower body. Picture the \/-shaped plane.

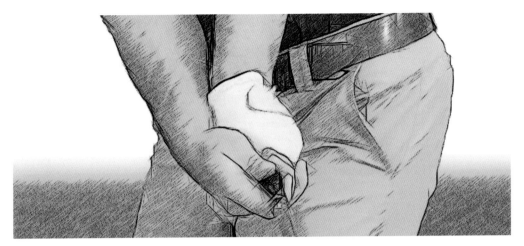

The right hand is under the left post-impact.

8. **FAULT:** Hitting hooks and blocks (the ball starts right of the target). These two faults are commonly referred to as being *too far underneath* or *stuck*.

FIX: Just like the relationship between a slice and a pull, the hook and block go hand in hand. Typically, better players suffer from these issues, which are caused when the club approaches from too far inside the target line. For right-handed golfers, if the club-face matches this in-to-out swing path at impact, the shot will be blocked and fly on a straight line right of the target. If the clubface is left or quite closed relative to this in-to-out path, the ball will hook left of the target on a curving flight. Good players often hit hooks as a result of trying to salvage a poor downswing path with some aggressive hand-and-forearm action. Sometimes they sense they are about to hook the ball and purposely hold the face open and block the shot. You want hand action in the swing, but it has to be the correct hand action. *The role of the right hand is key here. It should stay behind the left hand as the club meets the ball and then rotate under the left hand post-impact.* Eliminating excessive hand-and-forearm rotation encourages the club to be pulled through the impact zone on line and keeps the clubface squarer to the target through impact. Both result in better accuracy.

CHECK: That the right hand is back and behind the left hand coming into the ball and is then under the left after impact.

9. **FAULT:** Hitting fat and thin shots with your irons.

   FIX: For solid iron shots, it's essential to hit down on the ball—this imparts backspin, which gets the ball airborne. At impact, your body weight should predominantly be supported on your left side, with the shaft leaning toward the target. If you're not taking any divots, or if the divots are behind the ball, then you're most likely failing to get your weight onto your left side and your shaft is incorrectly leaning away from the target at impact. This often happens when golfers try to help the ball into the air with a scooping motion of the hands, or if they feel that they have to get the clubhead "under" the ball to get loft on the shot. Practice hitting shots where you emphasize taking a divot after the ball is struck. To get the sensation of what this type of swing feels like, you might find it easier to practice this by hitting short wedge shots on a slight downhill lie. Also place a little more weight on your left foot at address—particularly with your short irons—to help you to hit down on the ball.

   CHECK: That your body weight is supported by your left leg at impact. Your sternum must feel forward and in line with the ball (termed *covering* the ball), and your hands ahead of the clubhead (closer to the target) at the moment of contact.

10. **FAULT:** Poor tempo. Swinging too fast or too slow.

    FIX: A big key to repeatedly hitting the ball solidly in the middle of the clubface is tempo. No matter what club you're using when hitting a full shot, the swing should take the same amount of time from address to impact—the hallmark of good tempo. It's what keeps your swing consistent from club to club. Trying to consciously slow the swing down or speed it up with your arms and hands will greatly increase your chance of off-center hits. You must control the pace of your swing with your body pivot. *Swing the club no faster or slower than the pace of your pivot dictates—the arms and club should move in harmony with the body and give the swing a smooth appearance.* Pacing your swing with the pivot not only helps you deliver maximum power at the precise moment of impact, but it also keeps the club moving on a consistent path, which ensures center-face contact.

    CHECK: That the tempo of your swing is dictated by the pivot.

Within this list of fixes is the key to hitting it well again using the A Swing. Many of the fixes I recommend can help correct more than one fault, and my absolute favorite is the sidestep drill, which shallows the downswing plane during the transition. **Initiating the downswing with the lower body gliding toward the target is the magic move of all good ball-strikers.** When you sidestep toward the target with your left foot, you'll get a feel for what the lower body is supposed to do. The A Swing backswing is designed to make it easier for this magic move to take place. It sets up the correct downswing sequence with the lower body leading, followed by the upper body, arms, hands, and finally the club. Doing the sidestep drill will help you ingrain the feel of what happens when you transition from backswing to downswing. You can eventually graduate to hitting shots with this drill and incorporate the feel of it into your regular swing.

I believe the A Swing offers golfers a chance to play to their true capabilities. The reason lies in its simplicity—it's easy to understand and easy to learn. I realize most people don't have a lot of time to work on their game, so I've designed a practice routine that is quick and simple to follow and gets results. In our testing to develop the A Swing, we found that it required only a series of seven-minute practice sessions, two to three times a week, for golfers to benefit and develop that all-important muscle memory. That's right, you'll be done in only *seven minutes*—seven minutes to better golf, now there's a plan! You do these quick practice sessions indoors, and you don't hit any balls. You can certainly go to the range and hit shots to get

CHAPTER 7

THE A SWING SEVEN-MINUTE PRACTICE PLAN

some feedback periodically, which is obviously beneficial. But as you develop confidence in your A Swing technique as a result of these short concise practice sessions, you could actually now have time to spend on your short game and putting and really lower your scores as opposed to just wacking balls! The seven-minute plan consists of six A Swing exercises. Doing the program regularly will make the A Swing feel instinctive and natural—which it has to be to play your best golf. If you commit to this reasonable practice regimen, you'll no longer have to stand over the ball on the first tee and say to yourself, for instance, **What was that thought I had last week that seemed to work?** Getting the swing down is all about repetition—doing the same thing over and over so you can play without getting mechanical or overthinking and just build up a feel for it. Initially when you learn the A Swing, a bit of thought will be involved, but soon you will learn to play by instinct as a result of following the seven-minute plan and developing your muscle memory. I'm sure you can devote twenty-one minutes out of your week to work on it—especially with the rewards of better golf waiting for you.

THE PLAN

Do the following six exercises in sets of **ten repetitions,** in the order they are listed. You should have enough time to gather yourself in between the sets, but if you initially find it difficult to finish all six exercises in seven minutes, it's fine to reduce the number of reps in each set until you become accustomed to the program. These exercises not only will help you groove the A Swing, but also will get you stronger and more flexible. It's like a mini-workout!

If possible, do the program in front of a mirror and/or with a partner watching for instant feedback. When doing them in front of a mirror, change your angle of view from time to time to help confirm that the position you're in is actually the position you want to be in. Have your swings or motions filmed occasionally as well, and compare them to the illustrations in this book. I recommend doing these exercises with an 8 or 9 iron or my specially designed Short Club (see "The A Swing Training Aids" at the end of the book), ideal for practicing indoors.

A SWING EXERCISES

Keep the upper portion of the arms resting lightly against the chest as you lower the club.

1. **DEVELOPING A GOOD SETUP.** This is simply a review of what you learned in the "Foundation" chapter. Setting up with a ball fairly centered in your stance, adopt the prayer grip, stand tall in good balance, and hold the club up in front of you. Your legs should be straight and your arms resting in a relaxed manner against the sides of your chest. Now tilt your upper body forward from the hips, allowing the tailbone to move back while keeping your chest up and shoulder blades down. Allow your knees to soften a touch. Once you're tilted forward, bump your left hip up slightly, then lower your relaxed arms until the club is soled. The upper arms rest lightly on the chest, and the right arm should be a touch lower than the left. To complete the setup, move your right foot back a little so its toes are in line with the laces on your left shoe. Hold this position for a couple of seconds, then repeat (ten reps).

2. **GROOVING THE PIVOT.** In this exercise, let's rehearse our pivot motion as in chapter 4. Get into your address posture without a club, then cross your arms so your hands are gripping the opposite sides of your stomach as if you're giving yourself a hug. Pivot from start to finish in a rhythmical fashion without stopping at the top. Sense the pressure in the feet as we have discussed. It can help to have a ball in front of you to have an object to focus on. To enhance this drill, do it with your butt touching a wall throughout the pivot. Repeat (ten reps).

Preset the club and wind to the top to get into a perfect position.

3. **SLOTTING THE TOP OF YOUR BACKSWING.** Get into your setup and hold a club using the prayer grip. With your upper arms resting against the sides of your chest, hinge your wrists and raise the club until it's parallel to your spine angle. The shaft should be leaning slightly to the right to match the spine tilt you established in the setup. Use a mirror to check it. From this preset position, wind your torso as if making a normal backswing. Complete the move all the way to the top with the left arm maintaining contact with the upper torso. The arms need to feel relaxed, and all the emphasis must be on winding the torso and keeping the arm swing short. At the top, the club will be pointing slightly right of the target and the angles at the back of the wrists will be symmetrical, and the left arm will be lower than your shoulders. Repeat (ten reps).

Splitting the hands gives you a real feel for the A Swing.

4. **FEELING THE BACKSWING, SLOTTING THE DOWNSWING.** Get into your address position holding a club, but separate your hands on the grip so that they are about an inch apart—this builds awareness of the action of the hands and arms. You can put a ball down for reference purposes. Starting from address, make a backswing, checking to make sure you're in these correct positions in this order: (1) The left arm is close to your torso and moving across the chest. (2) The left wrist is cocked with a cup at the back of the wrist. (3) The right wrist is hinged so the palm is facing the ground. (4) The clubface is looking at the ball. (5) The clubhead is outside the line of the hands, but inside the target line. (6) The right arm is higher than the left. (7) The angle of the club gets close to matching the spine halfway back—one side of the $\setminus\!/$ plane. (8) The right biceps muscles are pinching the right chest muscle at the top. (9) The arm swing is short, the torso is wound. (10) The left arm is under the shoulders at the top. (11) The club is pointing slightly to the right of the target. Now you're ready for the downswing.

Just as you are completing the motion to the top, in a smooth movement glide your lower body toward the target so that the club shaft shallows and drops onto the other side of the $\bigvee$ plane. When you stop the swing just short of halfway down, with your left arm close to the chest, the club should be parallel to the original plane. Check this in a mirror by standing as if you were swinging away from your reflection. Place a piece of Plane Tape (see "The A Swing Training Aids" at the end of the book) on the mirror that matches the angle of the club shaft at address—the original plane. When you swing down and reach this checkpoint, make sure the club shaft is on a parallel line (not directly on it) with the tape on the mirror. Your body (hips and shoulders) should be aligned right of the target. Hold this position for a two count, then repeat the entire movement. Do this in a smooth but continuous pace and build awareness for the shape of the swing. Really sense the way you complete the backswing and start the downswing (ten reps).

With the left arm only, swing the clubhead back to halfway. Make sure the shaft is angled and then shallow it on the downswing and release the club into the follow-through.

5.   TRAINING THE PROPER LEFT-SIDE RELEASE. Grip the club about halfway down the handle with your left hand only or use the short training club and grab the left side of your stomach with your right hand (turn the club upside down if it feels too heavy). Keeping your left wrist in a cupped position, mimic a backswing by pushing the club

back with your left hand, arm, and shoulder. While you're doing this, pull on the side of your stomach with your right hand, which will help activate the core muscles and let them control the movement. Make certain that the butt end of the club is in close to your body and the clubhead is outside the hand. Swing it back to halfway only, checking that the shaft is angled on the $\backslash\!/$ plane (angled away from you).

With continuous motion, start forward with your lower body and feel how the club shaft makes a distinct shallowing motion to the other side of the $\backslash\!/$ plane—in other words, from steep to shallow. Keep rotating and clearing your body, allow the left forearm to rotate down, and let the club whip through the impact zone releasing into the follow-through. Your left arm stays close to the body through the impact area and then extends past the body before the elbow folds near the finish. At the completion of the swing, the left wrist should be in the cupped position it was in at the start. In fact, the only time during the swing when it's not cupped is at impact, when it's flat. Repeat (ten reps).

Do this exercise periodically holding the club upside down to work on increasing your clubhead speed.

6. **DEVELOPING FEEL.** The previous exercises covered all the parts of the A Swing—foundation, pivot, top of the backswing, transition, and release. Now it's time to put them together into one complete motion. The easiest way to feel and practice what the body, arms, and club are doing and how they sync up is to make full swings with your eyes closed. You will develop a great sense of flow, rhythm, and balance by doing this. Get into your address position and hold a club lightly with the prayer grip. Now initiate your backswing. Sensing the left arm is in close to the body and the clubhead is outside the hands, keep the arm swing short but make a full pivot at a smooth and steady pace. As you are completing the backswing with the arms and club, feel how the lower body starts to move toward the target. Also be aware of pressure in your feet as the weight transfers from the right heel into the front of the left foot. Now sense through impact your weight moving into the left heel and how the rotation of the body and the release of the arms and club are synchronized. The club should whip freely through the hitting area. The right

Practicing the A Swing with your eyes closed will help you feel all the correct positions as well as improve your rhythm and balance.

elbow and right hip, and the left elbow and left hip, work in tandem through impact. Swing to a balanced finish up on the right toe and hold this position for a second or two. Note the overall fluidity of the movement. Initially you might lose your balance doing this exercise, but keep doing it until it becomes effortless.

This eyes-closed exercise is good for improving overall feel. You can do it on the practice tee in between hitting balls or even on the course while you wait to hit your next shot. It's especially effective when your swing feels disjointed, out of sync, or lacks rhythm. Start doing this at half your normal pace and eventually increase to full speed. Doing this exercise regularly brings all the A Swing components together—building muscle memory and making the motion instinctive. You will develop a subliminal awareness for your swing, so your mind stays relatively quiet and you don't overthink it. That's the best state of mind to be able to play good golf. Repeat (ten reps).

A SWING FITNESS GUIDE

In addition to the seven-minute practice plan, I'm also including a simple, functional fitness routine that will help improve your strength, stability, and mobility. This short and easy fitness guide is provided to you by Trevor Anderson, who heads up the Leadbetter Dynamic Performance Program at our Academy World Headquarters at ChampionsGate in Orlando, Florida. This guide is designed to enhance the A Swing—especially if you feel you don't hit the ball as far as you should, lack flexibility, or have aches and pains after you play golf. Golfers who are stiff and tight, with limited range of motion, will benefit tremendously. Everyone can use the exercises as an activation program to get the muscles warmed up and ready for golf—it's important not to start cold. Just like the seven-minute practice plan, this routine can be done at home, before your warm-up, or you can even do some of them on the first tee before you start your round. It only takes a few minutes to cycle through the routine, and you don't have to do all the exercises if you're short on time. Trevor says to start off doing a limited number of repetitions of each exercise until you get used to them. Pay attention to your form. Once it becomes routine, you can do more reps and sets. Doing these exercises fairly regularly will help the cause and give you a general feeling of well-being. Having the ability to move freely as you get older, such as a Hale Irwin, Gary Player, or Sam Snead in his later years, will allow you to play good golf at an advanced age. Remember to start off slow—don't push it! Getting a little stronger, more flexible, and better balanced over a longer period is the goal.

EXERCISE 1—COUNTERBALANCE SQUAT WITH CLUB

PROCEDURE

- Start in a balanced position, feet shoulder-width apart, holding a club at each end with the shaft resting on top of the thighs.

- Keeping your heels on the ground and back straight, squat down until your hips dip slightly below the knees, or as far as you comfortably can—in time you will get lower! At the same time extend the club in front of your chest.

- Hold this position for a count of three and return to the start (if you struggle with this exercise initially, you can brace your back against a wall).

REPEAT (TEN REPS).

BENEFIT

This exercise strengthens and activates the muscles of the lower body (hamstrings, glutes, hip flexors, quads). You need lower-body stability to swing the club athletically and powerfully. You will be amazed how quickly your strength will increase in this area.

EXERCISE 2—GOOD-MORNING BOW

PROCEDURE

- Start in a balanced position, feet at normal shoulder width, and place a club on the upper part of the back just above the neck. If the club feels uncomfortable, simply fold your arms across your chest.

- While maintaining slightly bent knees, lean forward by bending at the hip joint (not your waist), making sure to keep the back straight and extended.

- Keeping the back as flat as possible, lower the chest toward the floor until the hamstrings are in a full stretch, hold for three seconds, then return to the starting position.

REPEAT (TEN REPS).

BENEFIT

This movement activates and stretches the hamstrings to relieve stress and relax the lower back, which is so important in making a good pivot.

EXERCISE 3—LOWER-BODY ACTIVATION

PROCEDURE

- Start in your golf posture, hips square, and extend your arms, placing the hands on top of a golf club in front of the body. Apply pressure on the club.

- While maintaining your golf posture, rotate/twist the hips as far as possible in each direction in a fluid motion while keeping the upper body still. Sense the movement through your core and feel the hips rotate back to the right, push forward to the target, and then rotate to the left. Return to the start.

REPEAT (FIFTEEN REPS, EACH DIRECTION).

BENEFIT

This movement is great for keeping the upper body stable while creating lower-body mobility and separation—great for loosening the hips and training the lower body to lead in the downswing. It enhances the transition in the A Swing.

EXERCISE 4—UPPER-BODY ACTIVATION

PROCEDURE

- Start in your address posture, but stand with one foot behind the other and your arms folded across the chest.

- While maintaining this posture, rotate as far as possible toward the foot that is in front, without losing posture or balance, then return to the starting position—right foot forward for backswing rotation, left foot forward for downswing rotation.

REPEAT (TEN REPS, THEN SWITCH THE POSITIONS OF THE FEET).

BENEFIT

This movement is great for establishing lower-body stability and balance, while increasing upper-body flexibility and rotation on a tilted axis. The exercise will maximize the winding and unwinding of the upper body on the backswing and downswing while you maintain your spine angle.

EXERCISE 5—ARM CROSSOVERS

PROCEDURE

- Start in a balanced position, feet shoulder-width apart, holding the club at both ends with the palm of the right hand facing up, and the palm of the left hand facing down. Keep the arms straight and extended in front of the chest.

- With the arms remaining straight, rotate the right arm over to the left side of the body, and then rotate and twist your torso to the left.

- Hold for three seconds and then return to the original position.

**REPEAT (FIVE REPS IN EACH DIRECTION,
THEN CHANGE HAND POSITIONS AND ROTATE THE OTHER WAY).**

BENEFIT

This movement engages, activates, and loosens up the shoulder muscles and helps increase torso rotation.

EXERCISE 6—OVERHEAD SIDE BENDS

PROCEDURE

- Start in a balanced position, feet shoulder-width apart, holding the club as high as you can above your head with both hands.

- While keeping your arms extended as far as you can, lean your torso to the right by bending at the hip joint (not the waist), making sure to keep the lower body relatively still.

- Side bend as far as you can without losing balance, hold for a count of three, and then return to the starting position.

REPEAT (FIVE REPS TO EACH SIDE).

BENEFIT

This stretch activates the upper body and prepares the oblique and lat muscles for a good pivot motion.

You'll notice that this functional-movement routine focuses on all of the major muscle groups around the middle of your body—especially your core. Having a strong midsection is key to hitting good golf shots, Trevor says. Strengthening muscles, freeing up joints, and increasing flexibility are not a necessity to perform the A Swing, but I think you'll find it will make it much easier, especially if you want to add distance to your drives! You might be amazed how your range of motion, strength, and speed increase—so important in golf, especially as you get older. You might hate the idea of exercising, but doing a circuit or two of these exercises a couple of times a week will help your golf game. So get fit—for golf!

FINAL THOUGHTS

I HOPE YOU ENJOYED READING this book and you're excited to give the A Swing a go. I realize a lot of information is here to digest, so I strongly recommend you learn it in bits—the foundation, the pivot motion, the arms-and-club movement, etc. If you reference the instructions, look at the illustrations from time to time, and do the seven-minute plan a few times a week, I think you'll pick up the A Swing fairly quickly. I'm excited about its prospects for helping golfers just like you. The results I've seen from students who have made the switch have been nothing short of spectacular.

You might have noticed that I've referenced some A Swing training aids. They help in the learning process. Go to www.leadbetteraswing.com to learn more about them and for the latest A Swing news and advice. Also, my instructors at the Leadbetter golf academies throughout the world teach the A Swing and will assist you in learning it. So you might want to visit one of my academies and book a session.

I'd like to leave you with this advice. When you give the A Swing a try, commit to it and be patient with it. I wouldn't be surprised if you hear from naysayers who criticize the A Swing and try to convince you that you're wasting your time trying it. But before you do that, ask yourself these questions: "Am I inconsistent with my current swing?" "Do I keep reverting to my same old bad habits?" "Do I have the capability to be a better golfer?" If you answer yes to any of these, then you have nothing to lose in trying the A Swing and taking the chance to breathe new life into your game. It is a different way of swinging the club—but it's not *that* different. If anyone notices the changes, they'll probably be more impressed at how you're hitting the ball rather than prone to critiquing the new look of your backswing. The A Swing is simpler and more efficient; more important, it's a logical approach—the standard approach to learning the golf swing needs a change.

My goal has always been to help golfers enjoy this great game and to play better. I'm always thinking in that regard. I was born to teach. That's the reason why after all these years I felt it was important to develop an alternative way to swing the club, which did not compromise what I have taught for the past three decades. I want to help those players who constantly struggle with the game, or who are not reaching their potential no matter their current level of play. This A Swing is the result of seeing so many frustrated golfers. It's also a product of working with the greats and getting their feedback as to what is effective and what isn't; experimenting and testing with a range of golfers; utilizing science; and having a desire to offer an alternative, simpler approach to the paradigm that has been taught for years.

I enjoyed developing the A Swing and writing this book. I hope you have fun trying it—you have absolutely nothing to lose and everything to gain. As the late Ely Callaway, the founder of the Callaway Golf Company, when referring to why golfers keep purchasing the latest golf equipment, famously said, "All golfers live in hope of playing better." The A Swing might just be your great hope!

Best wishes for good golf.

APPENDIX:
FULL SEQUENCE OF THE A SWING

ACKNOWLEDGMENTS

Many people have helped me with the final development of the A Swing and the assembly of this book. I'd like to thank the following:

My coauthor, Ron Kaspriske, for his diligent work and his attention to detail

My A Swing model, Ryan Blaum, who was willing to adopt the A Swing approach, has seen some tremendous benefits, and who I know is going to have a great future in the game

My photographer, Pete Simonson

My illustrator, Scott Addison

My assistant, Jessica Mazzer, who spent so many hours helping to get this book together

My longtime friend and brilliant biomechanist, J. J. Rivet

My director of fitness, Trevor Anderson. Great contribution, TA

My good friend Denis Watson, whose critique was invaluable

My students of all levels through the years who helped shape my thinking about the game

My A Swing test students, who were open-minded and gave me great feedback

All my proofreaders

My editor, Marc Resnick, of St. Martin's Press

CONTACTS

For all instructional information at our worldwide academies and A Swing product information, contact:

THE A SWING

WEB SITE: www.leadbetteraswing.com

E-MAIL: info@leadbetteraswing.com

THE LEADBETTER GOLF ACADEMY WORLD HEADQUARTERS

WEB SITE: www.davidleadbetter.com

ADDRESS: 8595 White Shark Boulevard, ChampionsGate, FL 33896 (USA)

TOLL FREE: 1-888-633-5323 (LEAD)

PHONE: 407-787-3330 (USA)

E-MAIL: info@davidleadbetter.com

TWITTER: @DavidLeadbetter

FACEBOOK: www.facebook.com/TheLeadbetterGolfAcademy

J. J. RIVET: Master of biomechanics

E-MAIL: jj-rivet@biomecaswing.com

TREVOR ANDERSON: Director of golf performance and master trainer, the Leadbetter Golf Academy

WEB SITE: www.leadbetterperformance.com

E-MAIL: trevor.anderson@davidleadbetter.com

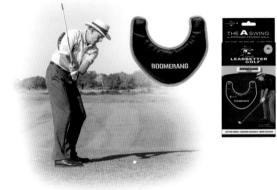

DAVID LEADBETTER is a leader and pioneer in the golf-instruction industry. He has coached players who have won nineteen major championships. He operates multiple golf academies around the globe and has authored several bestselling instruction books and videos. David writes monthly articles for the game's leading publication, *Golf Digest*. He lives in Sarasota, Florida.

RON KASPRISKE is a longtime editor at *Golf Digest* and has written five books on the game.

For additional A Swing resources, visit leadbetterAswing.com